I0139679

## Advance Praise for Putting Down the Paddles

*"I have had years of vast experience in metaphysics, energy healing, and shamanic studies. Throughout all my learning, I have found the simplified teachings that Susan M. Wright illustrates in* Putting Down the Paddles *to be the most powerful. Susan's techniques and applications have made both my personal and business life so much easier! Thank you, Susan, for putting things into perspective."*

~**Danielle Garcia, Intuitive, Spiritual Counselor, Medium, Channel, Author,** *Angel Blessings: A Collection of Channeled Messages from the Angelic Realm,* **and Founder of Intuitive Angels**

*"Susan M. Wright has delivered a beautifully appointed path to letting go. The journey includes lush rest stops and the time to take in the concepts she presents. The reader feels at once motivated and supported along the way."*

~**Peggy Ashman, Author,** *Inexplicable Grace: An Adoptee Journeys Home*

*"The lessons seemed simple and a little random at first but as I breathed deeply and contemplated each lesson each day, I was surprised how the lessons built on one another to shed light on areas of my awareness I had not realized were hiding in darkness. This book helped me to free myself from old beliefs and expectations that no longer serve me, allowing the joy of life to flow."*

~**Michael G. Wright, Author**
**michaelsmusings.net**

"Putting Down the Paddles *does a bang up job of embodying Susan's ability to act as a 'gateway' and assist brother humanity to flow through uncharted territory. This book is a portal that allows the reader to lunge beyond the snarls of a fair to middling existence, in a clear cut way. Bravo!"*

~**Mary Kay Buttery, Founder, Life Made Simple**
**http://www.sfgtd.com**

*"Just when I thought I had it all together, I was reminded that life and living is a continuous process of evolving into my destiny. After reading,* Putting Down the Paddles: 30 Days to Living in the Flow, *I realized I must learn to slow down, listen, really listen and allow myself to open up and receive the influences around me that are required to mold me into a beautiful vessel. What a comfort to know that I can begin this process at any time, and if I give myself 30 days to meditate and focus on the lessons in* Putting Down the Paddles, *more great things are bound to happen in my life.'"*

**~Gina Eleane Wood, Advocate for Girls and Young Women**

*"Susan's book is enlightening, enriching and inspiring. This book will speak to you no matter where you are on your journey and push you further down the river toward inner peace."*

**~Melinda Mendenhall Stimac**

*"I was surprised and pleased that every day's lesson in the book was so practical and relevant to my daily life. Now, when I feel myself struggling to make things 'work out' – I start the 30 days again. Day by day, my sense of calm and peace increases.* Putting Down the Paddles *is great advice!"*

**~Sue Adam, Senior Business Consultant**

*"Bravo Susan for synthesizing complex principles for acceptance, forgiveness and living in the present moment into simple, practical and very powerful tools for daily living in* Putting Down the Paddles. *The life lessons and stories woven through provide amazing reference points for inspiration and how to apply the daily lessons in our own life. This work is a powerful testament and blueprint that can easily get someone accelerated in 30 days! Wow!"*

**~Anne Moore, Senior Change Management Consultant and Licensed Avatar® Master**

*"I have found* Putting Down the Paddles *a very useful tool. It's deceptively simple but each time I read the book, it takes me to a deeper level of contemplation and understanding. With every read something new reverberates with me – an idea that I understand in a deeper way, something I am ready to hear and maybe wasn't before."*

**~Nan Carson, Labor Relations Manager**

# Putting Down the Paddles

## 30 Days to Living in the Flow

By Susan M. Wright

Love Your Life

For more information about this book or the author, visit:

**www.puttingdownthepaddles.com**
**www.beacon-of-life.com**

Love Your Life

Love Your Life Publishing
www.loveyourlifepublishing.com
ISBN: 978-1-934509-60-9
Library of Congress Control Number: 2012947498
Printed in the United States of America
First Printing 2012
Cover design: www.Cyanotype.ca
Cover Photo © Fotosearch.com
Editing by Gwen Hoffnagle

**Disclaimer:**

*This book is dedicated to the love of my life, Wolfgang.*
*Thank you for sharing this journey with me.*

# CONTENTS

# FOREWORD

Welcome to *Putting Down the Paddles: 30 Days to Living in the Flow.*

I'm a life coach, writer, and energy healer. Although I've written weekly articles for the past ten years, this is my first book. Clients and friends had been asking me for several years, "So when is your book coming out?" I didn't know quite how to answer them because I wasn't precisely sure what I should write about. After much discussion, meditation, and asking for clarity, the fog began to lift and the idea for the book emerged.

For many years, I've realized and shared that "my life is in the flow." I've helped my clients and friends discover the divine flow of life and how to become comfortable navigating the waters. I thought that if I wrote a book it should share the lessons I've learned and the tips and techniques that have assisted me and so many others. I wrote this book for two main reasons: First, to enable as many people as possible to live a great life. Second, to assist *myself* in gaining clarity on several of the lessons that I share. I wrote this book for both of us – for me, the writer, and you, the reader.

How did I reach this place of "living in the flow"?

My journey of self-discovery began about twenty years ago. My life wasn't awful, but I had a feeling in my gut that there was more to life than what I was experiencing. I had a great job, wonderful friends, and a loving and supportive family. The only relationship I was missing was a romantic one, but that wasn't what triggered my search. It felt like "something" was missing. I hadn't found it at work, at church, in social clubs, or even at the new-age bookstore. All those places were great, but it still felt like there was something more to this life than what I was experiencing.

In the many workshops and seminars I attended, teachers told me that to live the life of my dreams I should just start moving in the direction of my passion. It sounded reasonable, and even a bit wise, but I didn't have an identifiable passion. What should I do? "No problem," the teachers told me, "There are other teachers who will assist you in identifying your passion." So I went to a couple of "find your passion" seminars, but I was still unclear about what my passion was – and therefore not clear about how to start moving in its direction.

So here I am, after twenty or so years, and I still don't know what my passion is or how to begin moving toward it. But that's OK, because along the way I figured something out: I am an explorer of life. My passion, if you want to call it that, is living life – however it shows up – and finding ways to move gracefully and joyfully through whatever doors happen to open up for me.

This idea of passion as a goal or mission, or even a vision that I can move toward, does not resonate with me. I suppose I have short-term goals, but even those can be extremely flexible. At present, I'm very much a "show me what today looks like" kind of person. I'm sure it sounds like an easy life to live, and with practice and patience it can be. It can also be very challenging, and sometimes a bit lonely, because it's definitely outside the norm.

As I reflected on how I arrived at this understanding of my life and how I've become more and more comfortable navigating the waters, I realized that other adventurers might benefit from my journey. After all, everyone's life is a journey. Some journey toward a particular passion while others, like me, journey for the sheer joy of discovery. Either way, the journey becomes much more joyful and harmonious when we go with the flow of life rather than attempting to paddle upstream.

*Putting Down the Paddles: 30 Days to Living in the Flow* is a distillation of my key discoveries thus far on my journey. When I received the inspiration for this book, I sat in meditation and asked, "What is the main topic for each of the 30 days?" The topics came to me in a flash and I wrote them down, not knowing precisely how I was going to expand on any of them. Writing these daily lessons and asking for guidance and clarity has been a journey for me. I noticed that as the days went by, some lessons came easily while others caused me to dig deep, clear the blockages, and receive the guidance required to put "deep knowing" into words. I am deeply grateful for the opportunity to create this book and I thank you for joining me on my journey.

For readers of this book, I offer a *free* download of *Woo-Woo Wisdom: Inspirational Stories to Transform Your Life*. This PDF-format book contains some of my favorite "Weekly Wisdom" articles paired with favorite photos. Follow this URL to get your download now: www.PuttingDownThePaddles.com/readersonly.html.

Welcome again to these 30 Lessons. Enjoy the ride!

Susan M. Wright
susan@beacon-of-life.com

# HOW TO GET THE MOST OUT
# OF THIS BOOK

As you may have noticed, *Putting Down the Paddles: 30 Days to Living in the Flow* is not written as a "read through to the end and stop" book. It's written so that you'll pick it up each day for the next 30 days.

Read one lesson each day. Give yourself some time to consider the ideas presented. If you meditate, then read the lesson just prior to your daily meditation. You may want to consider keeping a journal to record your thoughts and experiences throughout these 30 days.

Don't worry if you read a lesson and you just don't "get it" or it doesn't resonate with you. Either the lesson doesn't apply to you or it doesn't apply to you at this moment in time. Embrace the lessons that resonate and set the others aside for now. You can always pick them up later when it feels right.

I've created a page on my website where readers can post their thoughts, ask questions, and read through the Frequently Asked Questions (FAQ). I'll update the FAQ periodically based on your questions and feedback. This will give you a place to take your experience "beyond the book." You can find this page by going to www.PuttingDownThePaddles.com/faq.html.

To make it simple to remember which lesson to read, choose the lesson that corresponds with the date on the calendar. If it's the first day of the month, read Day 1; the second day of the month, read Day 2, and so on.

After Day 30, you'll find an appendix that includes my "Tools for Living in the Flow." These were published a few years ago as a stand-alone booklet, but I felt that the lessons and tools were a perfect fit, so I included them here as a gift to you. I incorporated a few of these into the 30 Lessons. Look them over and use them whenever you find yourself feeling stressed, frustrated, overwhelmed, angry, or just "out of sorts."

Once you've completed the 30 Lessons, you may want to repeat the cycle once, or many times, as you fully incorporate these lessons into your daily life. You can repeat this series of lessons as long as you like, month after month, until you feel you are "complete" with the material.

You may not feel compelled to repeat the lessons, but you may want to revisit those that touched you the most or gave you the best benefit.

You can also use this book as an oracle. Ask the question, "What does the universe want me to pay attention to today?" Then open the book and see where you land.

The coaching I provide and the classes I teach are all geared toward assisting you with "living in the flow." To find out more about my services, visit my website: www.beacon-of-life.com.

# CHAPTER 1

## *What Is Living in the Flow?*

# Putting Down the Paddles

I'm sure you know, or have known, someone who can be described as easygoing – who just goes with the flow regardless of what life throws at them. This is an example of living in the flow. Some people are born with the ability to flow with whatever life hands them, while for others living in the flow is a skill that is learned, practiced, then mastered.

Perhaps the best way to describe living in the flow is by analogy. Imagine, if you will, that you live your life aboard a riverboat. Sometimes the river is smooth and easygoing, sometimes it runs fast, and sometimes you find yourself flying through the rapids, hoping you won't be smashed against a rock. If you're living in the flow, then you're flowing through all these stages of the river. You've learned to flow with ease, even when the ride isn't easy.

Living *in* the flow means going *with* the flow, *allowing* the river of life to take you where it will and *enjoying* the ride.

There are some who will read this and think it seems a bit defeatist. Living in the flow? Allowing life to take you wherever? Having no control over any of it? What about goals? What about dreams? Are we just supposed to give up on everything we've worked toward and just sit down and go with the flow? Not exactly.

Living in the flow involves understanding some subtle clues that can make the difference between the life of your dreams and a life of nightmares. My preferences, thoughts, and energies have some degree of influence on the flow. Without getting into all the details here, I'll say that I know that the Law of Attraction is always at work and I'm continually mapping out (consciously or unconsciously) the direction of the flow. The beauty is that the flow of life can, and does, bring me wonders beyond my conscious and unconscious thoughts. Learning to appreciate the unexpected and uncontrollable is key to my appreciation of life.

It sounds a bit contradictory – should we go with the flow, or create the flow? Which is it? Well, it's both. I can put forth where I want to go, but then I let the boat flow easily, knowing that I'm going to arrive where I said I wanted to go. I can also tell God and the universe to handle it, and only concern myself with what shows up in front of my boat each day.

For me, *living in the flow* means letting my past be my past, accepting life on its own terms, not attempting to change or control other people, and seeing the beauty of everything around me while knowing that I'm more than this body I inhabit and that everything I will ever need is provided by the universe. Whenever I'm guided to pick up my paddle and row, it's simply to steer my boat around an upcoming obstacle. I no longer attempt to paddle upstream against the current.

Sometimes I say to my clients, "Follow your guidance, go with the flow, and see where it takes you." And they think, "Ah, she's not being bold; she's not very passionate; she lacks focus and dedication."

What they're missing is this: Let me take you back to the river. Imagine you're on a rafting adventure, perhaps floating down the Arkansas River just outside of Leadville, Colorado. There have been many days of rain and the river is flowing quickly. Up ahead are class 4, maybe class 5 rapids. The sight of the rapids scares the wits out of you and you want to paddle with all your strength to the bank of the river so you can get out of the raft and walk around the rapids. Instead, your guide has you paddling directly into the rapids – right to the middle of the craziness. It's not easy, it's scary, but you were guided to take this ride today and you trust your guide, so you ride those rapids and come out on the other side, soaking wet, tired, adrenaline pumping, and loving life fully.

It takes dedication to ask for guidance, to follow guidance, and to ride the flow wherever it takes you. It takes moment-to-moment focus and long-term commitment to be an adventurer willing to go wherever life takes you – not fighting the changes, but rolling with them – seeing everything as perfect and everyone as a divine spark of God.

This idea of living in the flow is both easy and difficult. It will take you to places you never dreamed existed and introduce you to people you never would have encountered if you had maintained a laser-like focus on living the life that your ego-mind dreamed up for you.

Living in the flow is different for each person, but the common thread is that those living in the flow live with the attitude of *thriving in peace* rather than *fighting and surviving*.

# CHAPTER 2

*Ten Minutes a Day*

# Putting Down the Paddles

Each lesson is designed to take approximately ten minutes to read and contemplate. You may wish to keep a journal of your thoughts and ideas, and ways to apply each lesson.

Read one lesson a day – and do your best to live that lesson. Once you've completed all 30 Lessons, you can start over with Lesson 1 and see if your understanding of the lesson has changed. Often as we shift and grow, we see subtle bits of wisdom we didn't see in prior readings. If you don't wish to repeat each lesson, go back to the ones that resonated most strongly with you – or open the book to a random page and see what Spirit has in store for you today.

The ideas presented here are not new, as evidenced by the quotations I include with each lesson. These ideas and concepts have been taught for eons. This book is my way of distilling things down and putting these ideas and concepts into a prescription, if you will, for transforming your life. Entire books have been written about the topics I present. As I notice books that may be of interest to you in expanding your understanding of a concept, I'll list them on my website: www.PuttingDownThePaddles.com/recommendations.html.

# CHAPTER 3

*The 30 Lessons*

# Day 1

## *Accept Where You Are – Right Now – Today*

Acceptance is easy when life is going great. Heck yeah I accept that I'm healthy, have great relationships, plenty of money in the bank, and a job I love! Life is awesome!

But what if life is not awesome for you? What if life is not as great as you had hoped it would be? How do you get to the place where life is awesome?

That's the point of the next 30 days. When you're living in the flow, life is pretty darn good. You might still get hung up here and there, but the more you learn to live in the flow, the easier it becomes to get yourself unstuck and back in the flow.

So back to *today*.

Everything you've experienced in your life has brought you to this point. Most likely, you've experienced some amazing things along the way. Even if you're not exactly where you want to be right now, you cannot *change* where you are *right now*. You can change where you're going, but you have been where you have been, and you are where you are.

Embrace where you are, because you're alive! You have the ability to read these words and you have the curiosity to wonder where you might be going next. Humans are marvelous creatures with the capacity to create the most wondrous things. Celebrate your humanity – right now – today.

I understand that sometimes life is very hard. Sometimes it's difficult to get up in the morning and do what you need to do to get through the day. But ask yourself, "Is this really how I want to spend my time? Do I want the next moment to feel like this moment, or do I want something different for myself?" If you want something different, read on.

**Today's Message:** Be open to what is currently happening in your life. Regret is useful only as a tool to guide your future steps. Use your energy to recognize and step through the doors that the universe is holding open for you – today.

*"Sometimes we stare so long at a door that is closing that we see too late the one that is open."*

~Alexander Graham Bell

# Day 2

## *Breathe In This Wonderful Moment*

A re you reading this while listening to a conference call, with the TV on in the background, or while you're on the phone or an online chat session? If so, *stop*. Finish up everything else you're doing, and then – *breathe*. Take a deep breath in and out. Take another breath in and out. Let's go for a third breath – deeply in, and release!

Ah, now we're here, together, in this moment. You're here. My words are here. Our shared energy connects us. It feels wonderful!

Many of us are masters at multitasking. We can handle emails, phone calls, and even paperwork all at the same time. When we're doing something that comes easily to us, multitasking is no big deal. We get more done, we don't get bored, life is good. However, when we attempt to examine our lives, create our dreams, or learn new concepts – all while multitasking – we're shortchanging ourselves.

Whenever the day gets hectic and you feel like you might not be "all here," stop and take a breath, or two or three. Bring your attention back to the moment, gather your thoughts, and take the next step forward.

When you decide it's time to read the latest self-help book, say your daily affirmations, or design your next creation, make sure you're operating in the moment. *Don't multitask your dreams!* Stop... and breathe in this moment. Gather all of yourself together, take a deep breath, and read the book, say the affirmation, or design your creation.

**Today's Message:**   You deserve to give yourself your utmost attention.  Whatever concerns or worries you have, set them aside.  If you must, promise your concerns and worries that you'll be back to retrieve them.  Now give yourself the time for easy breathing, contemplating, and enjoying this wonderful moment.  Allow the moment to stretch into two, then five, or perhaps ten.  Just be for as long as you're comfortable, and then go about your day.

### *If you have trouble putting your concerns and worries aside, try this:*

Make a "worry jar."  Using a regular jar or other container, make a sign that says "Worries Go Here."  Tape the sign to the jar.  Write down your worries on slips of paper and put them in the jar.  When you decide it's time, take the papers out and use your time to contemplate your worries.  You'll find that most of your worries are no longer a concern.

If you'd like a more colorful solution, purchase a set of Guatemalan "worry dolls."   According to http://www.worrydoll.com, "The Guatemalan children believe that before you go to bed at night you tell one worry to each doll, put the dolls under your pillow, and when you get up in the morning your worries are gone."

*"I took a deep breath and listened to the old bray of my heart: I am, I am, I am."*

~Sylvia Plath

# Day 3

## *Cultivate Your Curiosity*

When we are little – around age two or three – we begin to ask, "Why?" – about everything. We are curious. We want to know how and why the world works the way it does. Adults try to answer our questions as best they can, but often the answers are simplistic. Does any adult actually try to explain to a three-year-old why the sky is blue? At some point in our childhood, we stop asking why and begin to accept whatever cultural norms we see around us.

The rules that guide our families and our culture often become the beliefs that rule our lives. There are always rebels, of course, but most of us create our beliefs based on what we've been told and what we observe in others.

For example, there are many messages in our culture that say we must work hard to "succeed." This brings up several questions for me. If our work is our passion, or is not hard, do we ever feel like we are a success? How often have you heard co-workers greet each other with, "Working hard – or hardly working?" How do I explain all the people I know who work hard every day but never quite succeed? How do I define *success*? The list of questions keeps growing!

Now is a good time to open Pandora's Box and begin to ask why, and why not? What are we questioning? Perhaps we should question everything we believe about the world and ourselves, because what we believe about life influences how we move through life.

What do you believe about yourself? Is that belief really true or have you made it true by believing it for so long? Perhaps you *are* good with numbers. Perhaps you *can* act or sing. On the flip side, perhaps you are *not* ugly. Perhaps you are *not* a victim, a loser, or whatever.

Who said, "Life is hard and then you die"? What nonsense! Life is what you make it.

**Today's Message:** Be curious about life. Who said that this or that is true? Why do they get to make the rules? Could it be possible that you've been given the wrong rulebook? Might it just be possible that there's more to life than what you've been led to believe? There's no need to throw everything out the window at once, but now is a great day to be *open to the possibility* that you can be, experience, and have more than you previously thought possible.

*"The sun shines and warms and lights us and we have no curiosity to know why this is so; but we ask the reason of all evil, of pain, and hunger, and mosquitoes and silly people."*

~Ralph Waldo Emerson

# Day 4

## *Celebrate What You Did Right Today*

Most people I've met in my life are very accomplished at noticing what they and others have done wrong. I doubt that I have to work very hard to convince you of this point. The question is, what did you do right today?

What if you began to notice what you did right today? How might that shift your attitude?

There have been, and continue to be, nights when I lie awake rather than falling into a restful sleep. I lie there thinking about the mistakes and missteps of my day and worrying about what I need to accomplish the next day. When I shift my thinking to what I did right that day, I fall asleep feeling good about myself and wake up ready to take on the day.

In addition to noticing what you do right, what might happen if you noticed what *other people* do right?

In a previous life experience I managed a department for a large corporation. One of the key lessons I heard from the management experts was "Reward the behavior that you want to see repeated." Yes, there were times when I needed to address behavior that I didn't want to see repeated, but overall, reward and praise seemed to cultivate a much more productive work environment than punishment and criticism. When I saw someone doing something great, and acknowledged it, the person was more likely to continue to strive for greatness.

As you become more comfortable noticing what you're doing right, it's a natural extension to notice what others are doing right. Since we tend to see more of what we focus on, you will begin to see many things going right. Now that's a nice way to spend your day!

Today is a perfect day to celebrate "the right stuff."

***Today's Message:*** Review your day and find something to celebrate. Consider starting a "right stuff" journal in which each day you acknowledge your successes, *however minor or major*. I call this my "Accomplishment Journal."

Today (and every day), preferably just before going to bed, make a list of the things you did well. Write about what went right, contributions you made to others – anything that ends your day on a high note. If you also keep a Gratitude Journal, add a page for accomplishments, either before or after your notes of gratitude. You'll sleep better and wake up feeling confident in yourself and in your ability to navigate your day.

Another great use for the Accomplishment Journal: When you're having a particularly tough day, feeling like you just can't do anything right, pull out your Accomplishment Journal to remind yourself that failure is only temporary and that you do something right every day.

*"I celebrate myself, and sing myself."*

~Walt Whitman

# Day 5

## *Forgive Everyone for Everything*

A common metaphysical concept is that there is no right or wrong – there just *is*. This makes forgiveness a funny thing, because if we believe that there is no right or wrong, then there is nothing to forgive. Yet part of the human experience is feeling your emotions. When someone says or does something that we find offensive, or that hurts us in some way, we feel the emotions of anger, resentment, or some other pain. It's often difficult to forgive someone for causing such pain.

If you step back and really consider the situation, you can see that holding on to these emotions is what is harming you, not the person you feel has wronged you. This is true whether you've been wronged by an individual, a group of individuals, or even an institution or business. You're the one feeling the anger, resentment, or the ongoing pain. What we hope to release through the act of forgiveness is this physical and psychological pain.

Assuming you follow this logic, you'll see a valid reason to forgive. But you may be having a bit of trouble actually doing so. You want to let go of your anger and resentment, but it's just not leaving. I have a tool for that. It's called the "Forgiveness Process," and it's one of my "Tools for Living in the Flow."

The Forgiveness Process is a simple way to invoke universal forgiveness and divine grace. I've used this tool many times for many different situations. There are the obvious situations, such as when someone I know has said or done something that causes me pain (physical and/or emotional). But the most interesting situations are more general and sometimes create the most amazing healing. For example:

1. A client had a challenge with a local utility company. He had called several times and spoken with several different people, and the challenge was not resolved. During one call, he was speaking to a woman and was not getting the assistance he needed. She put him on hold, and while on hold he did the Forgiveness Process for her and for everyone in the company. When she came back on the line, everything had shifted. She was pleasant and able to resolve his issue quickly.

2. A friend was attending a large business meeting. Early in the meeting she felt very uncomfortable with the group at large. During a break she did the Forgiveness Process for everyone attending the meeting. When she returned to the meeting, it was as if she was in a different group altogether. Everyone was friendly and she felt much more comfortable.

3. Years ago, I had a business meeting scheduled with someone whom I never seemed to get along with. Coming to any agreement was always a challenge, and meeting with this person was always exhausting. Therefore, I did the Forgiveness Process before going to the meeting. Did this person and I become the best of friends? No. However, this meeting and all future meetings became productive. There was now a level of trust and mutual respect that made it much easier to agree, and I was no longer drained after these business meetings.

I've found that there is always an energetic shift – for the better – when I do this process with at least a *smidgen* of sincerity. The more sincere I am when forgiving, the more miraculous the results. This process creates an energetic shift in you, allowing you to experience people and institutions in a more open and loving way.

To be frank, it may not magically make an untrustworthy person into a trustworthy one. But it does allow you to use your discernment when dealing with people, without judging them and taking on feelings of anger and resentment. On the other hand, it might transform some people. People are who they are, and sometimes when you interact with them in an open and loving way, they'll respond to this energy and be honorable with you (even if they continue to be dishonorable with others).

Just to be clear, this process is *not* about controlling or changing anyone's behavior. It's about shifting the energy within *you* to assist you in welcoming in more and more of the divine love, energy, and abundance that's available to you. The process can help you remain calm and peaceful in the midst of an emotional storm, as it clears feelings of resentment, anger, jealousy, or victimhood.

This process can also work miracles at family gatherings, and is a perfect relationship tool!

So what is the magical process that creates miracles?

## The Forgiveness Process:

Say the following silently, filling in the blanks with the name of the person, group, or institution you choose to forgive:

Father, Mother, God [or whatever higher-level energy you choose to invoke],
I forgive _____ for everything they have ever done
For everything they are doing now
And for everything they will ever do
*and*
I ["ask" or "command," whichever you prefer] _____ to forgive me
For everything I have ever done
For everything I am doing now
And for everything I will ever do.
Thank you, God.
It is done. It is done. It is done.

# The 30 Lessons

**Today's Message:** Forgiveness is divine. Forgiveness is really about you, how you feel, and what tension and stress you're holding in your body. Forgiveness gives you the beautiful opportunity to release resentment, anger, and victimhood. There is no *requirement* to forgive, but there is great reward for doing so.

*"I can forgive, but I cannot forget, is only another way of saying, I will not forgive. Forgiveness ought to be like a cancelled note - torn in two, and burned up, so that it never can be shown against one."*

~Henry Ward Beecher

# Day 6

## *Be Willing to Say, "Thank Goodness That Happened!"*

Hen you look back at your life, especially at an event that was very difficult for you to deal with, how do you feel about the event? I'm not speaking of events like the passing of a loved one, but those when you felt disappointed with the outcome and as though you had been mistreated in some way. Consider looking back at such an event now and saying, *"Thank goodness that happened!"*

I realize that today's lesson might be a tough one for you, but it's so freeing when you can let go of the negative emotions connected to some event in your past.

Let me share a little story...

I was driving home late one evening. A song on the radio took me back to my last night in Plymouth, Michigan. I was moving away from a man whom I loved deeply, and the song brought out all of my memories of our last moments together. (In case you're wondering, the song I heard was "Save Tonight" by Eagle-Eye Cherry.)

The next day I described this man and that night to a close friend. I told her how this man had embodied all the criteria on my list for the perfect mate and how easily we had been with each other. My friend asked me, "So whatever happened to him?" My answer was, "Thankfully, he broke my heart."

At the time of that heartbreak, I was devastated. But after some time had gone by, I could clearly see that he and I were not as well suited as I had imagined us to be. There were aspects of the relationship that I had overlooked in my eagerness to finally find the perfect mate. In reality, I could not thrive with him. However, I couldn't see that until time and distance had cleared the "crush."

This broken heart was not the first time, or the last, that I've heard myself saying, "Thank goodness that happened!" When I look back at my life and realize how each event has moved me along my path, I can find appreciation for all of the events in my life.

Today's Message: Allow whatever grief is residing in your heart to dissolve and dissipate. See your disappointments and heartbreaks as contributing to the higher understanding of your journey through life. Find true compassion for all that you've experienced, and then bless each experience for adding to the richness of your life.

*"Life can only be understood backward, but it must be lived forward."*
~Soren Kierkegaard

# Day 7

## *Open Yourself to Your Higher Realms*

Most people believe in some sort of higher power. Today's lesson is not about your religious beliefs. In my reality, you can be open to your higher realms and still maintain your beliefs about God or whatever higher power you worship.

Today is about becoming aware of, and opening yourself up to, the wisdom, power, and compassion of the universe. I call this "opening to your higher realms."

When I use the word *higher*, I'm not speaking of elevation in the sky or heavens. I'm not speaking of a realm that's better than the realm we currently occupy. The realms I'm referring to are more than me-in-my-body. I'm speaking of a part of me and a part of the universe that are not easily comprehended by the mind.

What do I perceive when I connect with my higher realms? The best description I can come up with is this: a blend of intuition, synchronicity, luck, psychic abilities, miracle healing, unconditional love, compassion, and curiosity, combined with the critical thinking of my mind. When I'm connected to, and communicating with, my higher realms, all these attributes, and more, are available to me.

I know that it may sound like a religious belief, but for me there's a subtle difference. I don't have to believe any of this to sense and feel it. I perceive no particular dogma. When I'm tapping in to my higher realms, I'm tapping in to the energy and consciousness of the entire universe.

How do I connect with these realms? Here are the general steps I follow:

**Step One:** I'm open to the possibility that there's more to me and the universe than I can perceive with my physical senses.

**Step Two:** I'm willing to experience a connection with my higher realms.

**Step Three:** I command the voice of my ego-mind to remain silent while I connect with my higher realms.

**Step Four:** I ask for the connection. I ask for guidance, clarity, and answers to my most perplexing questions – and then listen to what pops into my mind. I ask a yes or no question and see which answer jumps to my mind first – often before I've completed the question. If you prefer to pray, then pray and see what answers come to you. *Whichever tool you use, remember that asking is an important but often forgotten step.*

**Step Five:** Play, play, play. The more you practice asking questions and receiving answers, the easier it becomes. Practice with non-critical questions first to give you a feel for hearing that yes or no answer. "Should I leave extra early for work today?" "Is today a good day to shop for new shoes?" "Is this a good day to wash my car?" When you practice with questions that are not life changing, you'll feel more confident when asking for guidance on questions that could impact your life.

These are the steps I use and follow when coaching a client on this topic. If you're open to it, play with it. The more you play with this, the stronger the connection becomes.

# Putting Down the Paddles

***Today's Message:*** From William Shakespeare's *Hamlet*:

HORATIO. O day and night, but this is wondrous strange!
HAMLET. And therefore as a stranger give it welcome.
     There are more things in heaven and earth, Horatio,
     Than are dreamt of in your philosophy.

*"Ask and it will be given to you, seek and you will find, knock, and it will be opened to you."*

~ Matthew 7:7

# Day 8

## *Cultivate Compassion*

What is compassion and why is it worth cultivating?

The dictionary definition of *compassion* is "a feeling of deep sympathy and sorrow for another who is stricken by misfortune, accompanied by a strong desire to alleviate the suffering."

So compassion is not only feeling sympathy and sorrow for the ill fortunes of another, but also a strong desire to alleviate the suffering *even if that's not possible*.

For me, to feel compassion does not require seeing another person as a victim or as powerless. Instead, compassion is seeing that another person is in physical or emotional pain, and having a desire to assist them out of that pain.

Do I always fulfill my desire? No. Whether it's because I don't have the skills or resources required to alleviate their pain or because the person doesn't want my assistance, there's often nothing tangible that I can do. However, I can always send them love and light and a prayer for the quick relief of their suffering.

I need to keep in mind that what I perceive as "suffering" may be exactly the life path that person chooses to follow. I do my best to keep an open mind about this, and I council you to do so as well.

Why is it worthwhile to cultivate compassion? When I can feel compassion for others, I can also feel compassion for myself. And when I'm able to assist others in reducing or releasing their pain, it gives me a feeling of contributing to a higher purpose.

I'm not here to save the world. I'm here to live as joyfully as I possibly can. I'm here to address the challenges that present themselves, to allow things to be what they are, to see through as much manufactured drama as possible, and to find the beauty and perfection that resides wherever I happen to find myself. Above all, I'm here to incorporate all this peace, joy, beauty, and perfection into my day-to-day existence. Cultivating compassion for my fellow travelers helps me move along on my journey.

**Today's Message:** Some people have the skills and knowledge to navigate through anything that life throws at them. Other people do not. If you can assist someone in navigating the waters of life, then why *wouldn't* you do that?

*"Our task must be to free ourselves from this prison by widening our circles of compassion to embrace all living creatures and the whole of nature in its beauty."*

~Albert Einstein

# Day 9
## *Open Your Heart*

What does an open heart have to do with living in the flow? When I say, "Open your heart," I'm saying to open it to everyone – every shape, size, color, nationality, gender, and religious or political persuasion. Open your heart to family, friends, lovers, and enemies.

Since we're learning to live in the flow, think about a river. Imagine if a river said, "I'm fine with having to flow around rocks and boulders; I expect them to be here. But those tree stumps and beaver dams? Don't get me started!" Sounds silly, doesn't it?

That's how silly we sound when we close ourselves to any particular person or group of people based on some aspect of their being. Perhaps these people have just the right thing to offer that will make your life journey flow more smoothly. If you do not allow them into your life, in whatever small way, you'll never know.

I can understand when someone is closed to a particular person based on a past experience with them. Forgiveness is divine, but sometimes your gut tells you to stay away. Sometimes your guidance tells you that this person's energy is not of service to you. In those cases, I do my best to open my heart – from a distance. I keep an open heart and send them love and light.

Another aspect I want to talk about is your ability to open your heart in "receiving mode." There is a mistaken belief that an open heart is all about giving. While being generous with your love, your ideas, your compassion, and your gifts are all aspects of an open heart, giving is only half of the equation. The other half is receiving.

How open is your heart when people wish to give to you? How readily do you accept love, compassion, and forgiveness from others? How easily do you accept gifts? How open is the "In" door of your heart?

When your heart is fully open and you are sending love out and receiving love in – in whatever form the love takes – then your entire being becomes infused with love, light, and goodness. When you move through your day with an open heart, obstacles become opportunities for sharing and creativity.

**Today's Message:** Flow through life with an open heart. Yes, it might get scratched and bruised, and perhaps even broken, but if you keep your heart open it will quickly mend itself.

*"There is more hunger for love and appreciation in this world than for bread."*
~ Mother Teresa

# Day 10

## *See Yourself through the Loving Eyes of Others*

Today involves the assistance of other people in your life. Today is about seeing yourself through the eyes of the people who love, admire, and respect you. These people will help you see the most positive aspects of yourself.

Many years ago – sometime in the eighties – I was working for a very forward-thinking company. This company was open to providing its employees with experiences that would build their skills (leadership, communication, etc.). For ten weeks one autumn I was "on loan" to the local United Way through a program called "Loaned Executives."

I, along with about fifteen people from other local companies, worked exclusively for United Way during their main fundraising period. We remained on our company's payrolls, but we focused entirely on the United Way campaign. The hours were long, the assignments were stressful, and the fifteen of us had to rely on each other for help if we were to have any hope of succeeding at our tasks. It was probably the hardest I've ever worked and the most fun I've ever had at work.

At the end of these very intense ten weeks, we spent an afternoon saying goodbye. During that afternoon we completed an exercise. Each of us received a sheet of colored paper with our name written

29

at the top. The paper had a hole in each corner with a ribbon tied on, making a loop that allowed us to wear our papers like backward necklaces (the papers hung on our backs). With felt-tipped pens in hand, we wrote on each other's papers what we most admired, appreciated, and would always remember about that person. We wrote from our hearts.

After the exercise, I took off my pink sheet of paper to find it filled with the most loving words! In reading what my co-workers had written, I was able to see myself through their loving eyes. I could see myself as competent, knowledgeable, creative, determined, caring, trusted, and fun.

I had my paper laminated and have kept it with me through the years. It's always in an office drawer, and whenever I'm feeling a bit down, I pull out my laminated pink paper and see myself through those loving eyes. What an amazing pick-me-up!

**Today's Message – an assignment:** Ask five friends to write down and share with you what they most admire about you. Put these documents in sheet protectors (or have them laminated) and put them where you can easily see them. If you work in an office and don't want them hanging on your wall, put them in a drawer that you open frequently. Make sure these documents stay at the top of the drawer. Read them as often as possible, especially when you begin to doubt yourself.

*"Tell me who admires you and loves you, and I will tell you who you are."*
~Charles Augustin Sainte-Beuve

# Day 11

## *Release Your Fear*

When I speak of releasing fear, I'm referring to the fear that prevents you from following your heart's desire. Wouldn't it be amazing to face a wild animal or a mugger with no fear? Sure. But I'm not suggesting that I'm the teacher to take you there, at least not at the moment. However, I can assist you in releasing the fear that prevents you from living your life fully.

In my day-to-day life, I embrace the following definition of *fear*: *"False Evidence Appearing Real."*

Fear is rooted in the future. What if I go on stage and make a fool of myself? What if my business proposal is denied? What if I fail my test? What if? What if? What if?

When the "what if" questions emerge, ask the "did I" questions. In other words, "Did I practice my lines?" "Did I prepare?" "Did I do my homework?"

Sometimes a bit of fear is a great motivator to help you achieve something. Still, even if you answer all the "did I" questions with "Yes," you might fail at this particular endeavor. Failure is nothing to fear, especially if you can learn from it. Failure has been a consistent ingredient in the lives of most, if not all successful people. It has certainly been an ingredient in my life.

When fear rears its ugly head, other questions to ask yourself are: "How important is this?" "In what way might I avoid a bad outcome?" "Is there really something to fear here or is this all in my head?"

Sometimes, if the fear is massive, I employ a rather extreme method to alleviate it. When I find myself asking the "what if" questions, I play a little game. I envision the absolute worst-case scenario. For example, if the fear is about finances, I might ask, "What if I lose all my money, have no job, have no place to live, and have no car or other means of transportation? What if I become homeless and have to live on the streets?"

I can take this game to the extreme degree of *"What if I die?"*

You know what I've discovered? Even if I die, I know I'm eternal. I'm a spirit residing in a physical body for a short time. If the body dies, I still exist.

The chances of the worst-case scenario happening are extremely low. Yet if I can see myself going through the worst-case scenario and still existing, I'm pretty sure I can move through whatever life throws at me.

Now that you've allowed your mind to play with the fear, evidence, and possible outcomes, stop and take a breath. Bring your mind back to this moment. Here you are, alive and well, reading these words. There's nothing frightening here. Show appreciation for the preparation your fears have inspired and allow yourself to focus on your heart's desire. Give strength to your desire. See yourself enjoying the journey that moves you toward your desire.

**Today's Message:** Life is not about the achievement of any particular dream, but rather the journey toward that dream. When you truly understand this, you'll see that there's never anything to fear.

*"We are more often frightened than hurt; and we suffer more from imagination than from reality."*

~ Marcus Annaeus Seneca

# Day 12

## *Mind Your Ps and Qs*
## *(Please and Thank You)*

I remember spending time with a friend and her three-year-old little girl many years ago. Each time the little girl would ask for something, my friend would ask, "What's the magic word?" The magic word for asking was *please* and the words for receiving were *thank you*. Please and thank you.

Generations have taught these words as part of polite society. Is it possible that the power of please and thank you goes beyond politeness and actually enters the realm of magic? How many stories have you heard about people who fell as far as they possibly could and then – and only then – did they say, "Please help," and with that plea, their life began to improve?

What if we began each day with "Please, God, show me what's in store for me today. Help me to love, not judge. Please guide me through my day."?

To me, it feels like the energy of the word *please* is very powerful. While I'm not a numerologist, I checked the numerology of the word *please*. If I followed the chart correctly, the letters add up to the master number of 22. People with the number 22 are very powerful; they are "master builders."

By invoking the word *please*, we can tap in to that power. It indicates that we're asking for assistance. Each power in the universe would love to assist us with anything and everything we could possibly desire – yet we often forget to ask.

I've found that help shows up when I ask for it, and usually not until I ask. Perhaps the universe is following the same rule given to me when I first began my coaching career. I learned to provide assistance only when asked. I may see a friend going down a road that is not serving them, but I believe in free choice. The road they're on is only a detour, and they might be having fun with it. Actually, to say that a choice is not serving you is only *my* judgment. You can see why I do my best to provide assistance only when asked. If the universe is following this same guideline, then a "Please help!" to the universe or God is clearly a request, and it will be answered.

Of course, when you receive assistance, it's both polite and powerful to say, "Thank you." Many times each day I hear myself saying, "Thank you, God" for something or other. I say thank you for the guidance to assist a client, finding the perfect word to express a thought, a nice meal, and even having fun with friends. I have an amazingly blessed life, and I often find myself saying thank you for no reason, and for every reason.

"Thank you" says that you acknowledge receipt of what was given. When shopping for birthdays or Christmas, I love finding the absolute perfect gift to give. When I do stumble upon an amazing gift, I feel so happy giving it. It's not often that I hit a home run on my gift giving, but every once in a while I find something perfect. The "Thank you" I receive says that my intuition was correct, and I can keep my eyes open for the next wonderful gift to give that person.

God and the universe would love to give us whatever our hearts desire. It's up to us to remember to ask for assistance, say thank you when it's given, and clarify our requests to ensure that the universe is providing us with the tools to enjoy life fully.

*Please* and *thank you* – three words that carry immense power.

**Today's Message:** Practice asking for what you desire using *please* as the introductory word. Be sure to say "Thank you" when you receive what you've asked for. Be especially gracious when saying thank you for those unexpected gifts – the blessings that show up without our having asked for them.

*"I can no other answer make, but, thanks, and thanks."*

~William Shakespeare

# Day 13

## *Release Your Victimhood*

Today's lesson is a tough exercise for many of us. Many spiritual teachers tell us that we're the creators of our lives, but that's a difficult thing to accept when something horrible happens to us. So what's going on here?

I believe that we live on the planet of free choice. When something bad happens to me, I have some choices. I can go full tilt into "I create my own reality" mode and try to figure out how I created something so horrible. I can conclude that some people are evil and will always do evil things and that I was unlucky enough to have crossed paths with an evil person. I can assume that there's a gift in every bad circumstance and spend hours, days, and weeks searching for the gift.

I've done all of the above at some point or another, and there is value in each reaction. It's helpful to see how I might have been involved in creating an event, and it's magical to find a gift in a bad circumstance. I'm still undecided on the "some people are evil" choice, but I can see instances in which it's difficult to come to any other conclusion. However, what really works for me now is to look at the bad circumstance and conclude that what is, is. I'm in charge of *my reaction* toward a perpetrator, but I do not control the perpetrator.

Someone posted a picture on Facebook with a caption that read, "Holding a grudge is letting someone live rent-free in your head." The same is true of being a victim. Are you a victim of your gender? Of your religious beliefs? Of your background? Are you a victim of a crime? Holding on to feelings of victimhood allows your tormentor to live rent-free in your head. Assuming that you see value in the exercise, how do you release your victimhood?

Using the Forgiveness Process, begin by forgiving the perpetrator(s) for whatever they did. Then allow the past to be the past. I'm not telling you to deny what has happened in your life; I'm asking you to consider setting it aside and moving forward as an empowered individual rather than as a victim.

Something happened in your life that gave you the feeling of being victimized. It might have been something small or something big. For the purpose of this exercise, the severity of your victimization doesn't matter. What matters is whether you continue to carry that feeling of being victimized.

It's possible to say to yourself, "Yes, in that moment I was a victim – but I don't have to remain a victim. In that moment that thing happened, but it's not happening here in this moment. I release this event to the past and I choose to go forward, focusing on what is right in my life, determining what I can do to assist others, and understanding that I cannot only survive this event, I can thrive beyond it."

Forgiveness and letting the past be in the past are the first steps to becoming the empowered *you* that you always knew yourself to be. Release your victimhood. You're not denying your past; you're moving beyond it.

You're giving the ultimate thumbing of the nose to your tormentor when you say, "Yeah, you did that – but so what? I'm eternal and there's nothing you can do that can harm the real me. You may harm my body or mess with my mind, but you cannot touch my soul, my spirit, or my consciousness. I will not be a victim for you. I release you from my head."

**Today's Message:** Don't allow anyone to live rent-free in your head. Forgive them. Release traumatic events to the past, taking with you only the lessons learned and the gifts of strength and resilience.

*"Give light, and the darkness will disappear of itself."*
~ Desiderius Erasmus

# Day 14

## *Listen to Your Gut*

We've already talked about opening yourself to your higher realms and asking for their guidance and assistance. Now it's time to recognize and acknowledge that you've been getting guidance your entire life – even when you haven't asked for it. I call this "listening to your gut."

When you're about to do something that's not in your best interest, or does not serve the highest good of you and others involved, don't you feel a bit of a twinge in your gut? Isn't there a bit of a tightening and uncomfortable feeling in your belly? What might happen if you stopped right then and reconsidered your actions or your words? What might happen if you adjusted your behavior, however slightly, until that twinge in the gut went away?

This gut feeling is a physical manifestation of your intuition. Intuition is the direct line to guidance. Some people don't feel the twinge in the gut but they have some other physical symptom. I refer to the gut because most of us can relate to that feeling. Most of us have felt that twinge, have gone ahead with our plans anyway, and have later looked back and realized that we should have listened to our gut. The feeling is sometimes very subtle, very light, and sometimes is there for only a few seconds – but if we're honest with ourselves, we can feel it.

Here is the sort of thing that happens when I ignore my gut feelings:

Many years ago, when I was in my twenties, I dated a man who was in no way for my highest good. To be honest, I think I felt sorry for him and just didn't have the skills to assist him without trying to fix him. He wasn't in my life for very long, but my gut repeatedly told me that he was not the man for me. For some reason, I kept overriding my gut until I couldn't ignore it any longer.

I asked this man to leave my life and, after hitting bottom, he was just fine without me. I heard about him a few years later and learned that he had turned his life around and was doing really well. My feeling sorry for him had been holding him back. He needed to be on his own in order to make the changes that improved his life. My gut knew this, but it took time for me to listen.

Here's what happens when I listen to my gut:

It was a sunny Friday afternoon in the late 1970s. I was living in an apartment in Lawrence, Kansas, with my then-husband. We didn't have a laundry room at the complex, so I went to the laundromat each week. I usually did this on Friday afternoons, after my husband left for work.

On this particular Friday afternoon, I started to gather up the clothes, and my gut stopped me. I listened. I could not get myself to go to the laundromat. A couple of hours later, the tornado sirens went off. A tornado touched down on the edge of town, destroying the laundromat that I frequented. Listening to my gut saved my life.

**Today's Message:** Sometimes intuition is about something minor. Other times it's life or death. Always remember, your gut has your back! Listen to it.

*"The intuitive mind is a sacred gift and the rational mind is a faithful servant. We have created a society that honors the servant and has forgotten the gift."*
~ Albert Einstein

# Day 15

## *Create Your Bubble*

We live in a world that's in constant motion and frequent turmoil. As we open our hearts and connect with our higher levels, we may find that we become more sensitive to everything going on around us. We may feel that we just want to crawl into our cave and hide out.

Not long ago, at a dinner with friends, the conversation turned to politics. In my earlier years, I would have had a great time sharing my thoughts and hearing the (often dissenting) opinions of others. However, things are not as congenial as they were twenty years ago, and this discussion quickly turned ugly.

I made the mistake of sharing a positive opinion about a particular politician, and our most outspoken friend really let me have it! She very powerfully told me how horrible this person was and the awful things he had done.

I had to take a break, so I excused myself and went to the restroom. My head was spinning, and I felt pressure in my forehead and buzzing throughout my body. I was exhausted from a five-minute exchange. I really didn't want to go back to the table and resume such a hostile conversation. So I forgave my friend for her attack (using the Forgiveness Process), and commanded a Bliss Bubble to surround me.

When I went back to the table, I was able to steer the conversation to a new, more gentle topic. With the help of the Bliss Bubble, I was able to allow any attacks to flow past me – ignored and forgotten.

I like this bubble because it's not a shield that puts up a wall around me. It allows love and light to flow easily in and out of it, so it protects me from the "slings and arrows," but my interactions with people are maintained. The funny thing is, whenever I feel I've outgrown the need for a Bliss Bubble, something comes up and I need to create my bubble again.

When I think of the Bliss Bubble, I envision a scene from Star Trek. The captain is on the bridge and an enemy is on his screen. The captain gives the command "Shields up!" and the entire ship is protected by an invisible force field. Missiles shot at the ship cannot penetrate this invisible shield, but productive communications can.

The Bliss Bubble is a form of personal shield – an energetic field surrounding my body that allows only love and light to penetrate it. Only love and light can come into the bubble, and only love and light can go out.

## Invoking the Bliss Bubble:

Envision a shield around your body, like an invisible bubble with you at its center. Command that only love and light can move through this shield; only love and light can come in and only love and light can go out.

### Example:

"Father, Mother, God, I command that only love and light can come in through this shield and that I emanate only love and light to everyone and everything around me. Thank you, God. It is done."

**Today's Message:** The Bliss Bubble allows only love and light to move in and out of it. Sometimes when you're feeling a bit sensitive, you can use a little help in functioning. The Bliss Bubble helps you move through your day without building a wall between you and the world.

*"Nobody can hurt me without my permission."*

~ Mahatma Gandhi

# Day 16

## *Expand Beyond Your Bubble*

Yesterday's lesson is about protecting ourselves – when needed. Perpetually living in a bubble, even one that allows in love and light, can begin to feel isolating. So today seems like a good day to talk about moving beyond your protective bubble.

I didn't come to this planet to live in a cave, and I don't want to become dependent upon a tool such as the Bliss Bubble. Sure, this tool works miracles and brings peace. However, when that peace is achieved, it's time to expand beyond the bubble and engage with the bumps and the rapids that pop up in this river of life. When I no longer judge bumps as bad and peace as good, then I can cherish and engage with all of life.

Whenever I'm centered in myself, connected to my higher levels, and firmly grounded in this moment, protection is not an issue. When I'm in this connected space, I'm fully capable of moving gracefully through the day and assisting others who are having a bit of trouble with grace. From this space I can expand my consciousness throughout a room and energetically hold everyone in my welcoming arms.

To expand my consciousness, I take a deep breath in, and, with that breath, pull in as much of my essence as I can. I fill my body with the essence of pure consciousness. As I breathe out, I expand this essence (or consciousness) beyond my physical self to fill the room, and then the surrounding building, town, state, and continent. I expand my essence as far as I can comfortably do so. In this field of consciousness, I am who I am. I'm vibrating at the frequency of pure consciousness – beyond love, beyond light, and beyond anything my words can describe. I'm not *one with all that is*, but I'm *existing in harmony with all that is*.

To be sure, this takes practice. For today, I ask you to try the following: As you exist inside of your Bliss Bubble, envision pure consciousness, pure God energy, pure chi – whatever you wish to call it. Envision that nectar of the gods flowing through your body, aura, and Bliss Bubble. Now envision it flowing out of your bubble to touch everyone you connect with today.

**Today's Message:** The Bliss Bubble is an excellent tool when you need or desire a break from everything that's being thrown at you. As you become more comfortable with your own energy and vibration, you can begin to expand beyond the bubble and touch others with your gentleness and peace of mind. You can expand beyond your bubble to see life for what it is, with appreciation for the struggles and the gifts.

*"Here is the world. Beautiful and terrible things will happen. Don't be afraid."*
~Frederick Buechner

# Day 17

## *Identify Your Influencers*

Who do you listen to? What do you watch? How do you feel when you interact with others? Everyone you encounter has the potential to affect how you feel today. Some people have a greater impact on you than others. These interactions influence your actions, words, votes, and opinions. Who are these influencers? Do they really have your best interest at heart?

Think about who influences you the most. Is it your family? Your friends? An author you've read? A favorite teacher? A particular news program or website? Without judging them as good or bad, helpful or harmful, think about who influences you the most. Do you always accept what these people tell you, or do you question them?

I'm heavily influenced by my upbringing. My parents, my early religious education, and my teachers all had significant influence on who I am today. As I've moved along my path and grown in my journey, I've questioned many of my assumptions.

For instance, my parents taught me to work hard, be fair, have compassion, always pay my bills and taxes, put my children first above all others, and live with integrity and honesty. As I've grown, I've realized that hard work – for the sake of working hard – adds nothing to my life. However, serving my purpose does not feel like hard work. Others might look at me and say, "Wow, she works really hard!" I don't feel that way. I guess you'd say that I work for reasons other than fulfilling my earthly duty to work hard.

Still, if I need money I'll take almost any job in order to make the money to pay my bills. I don't care if it's a fast-food job or a greeter at Walmart. The influence of my parents has given me the willingness to do what it takes to live, and I've been blessed with the opportunity to do what I love.

Think about who or what influences you the most, and begin to question the rules, assumptions, and judgments that have come through those paths of influence. Do they still fit you? Are they true? Are they *your* truth?

Today is not about changing any of your beliefs or assumptions. It's about expanding your awareness. Once you become aware of what drives your thinking and decision-making, you can explore your beliefs and assumptions to determine whether or not they still serve you.

Let me give you an example. I've always heard that successful relationships take work. There are books, movies, and TV shows based on this idea of working on your relationships. There are also many messages in our society that say that work is no fun – it's a necessary evil. If I were to accept and agree with both of these beliefs, why would I ever want to be in a relationship? This awareness prompts me to question my assumptions. Who says that work has to be drudgery? Who says that you have to work on relationships?

By identifying who or what influences me, I gain awareness of the source of my beliefs. Awareness leads to questioning, and questioning will either strengthen a belief or give me the opportunity to release it.

**Today's Message:** Consider who and what influences you. Is that influence making your life better? Are you happier? Do you feel more at peace? Or does that influence cause you distress, upset, and judgment against others? You get to choose how you want to feel each day.

*"We all take different paths in life, but no matter where we go, we take a little of each other everywhere."*

~ author unknown

# Day 18
## *Release Old Connections*

Have you ever found yourself in the following situation? You're going through your day, feeling good about yourself, then suddenly something happens to remind you of a person or situation that makes you feel awful. This is especially frustrating when the person or situation is something you thought you had dealt with long ago. Sometimes these memories put me into a spiral of bad feelings and it becomes hard to dig myself out of the hole. I call these memories "connections that do not serve me."

Perhaps these connections served me at one time in my life, but they bring nothing helpful to my life now. So what do I do? I cut the cord.

I have a couple of tools that I use for this, which I'll lay out below. The important thing is that I release these connections from my life. When I become aware that an old connection to a person, place, job, or whatever is only serving to bring me down, I release that energetic connection.

The first tool is a prayer to Archangel Michael for "disconnecting":

*Archangel Michael,*
*Bathe me in the blue light protection of God*
*And with your blazing sword cut all of my connections*
*to everyone and everything.*
*Burn root, branch, and seed of every negative connection I have*
*and leave everyone and everything blessed.*

*Thank you, Michael.*
*It is done. It is done. It is done.*

If the prayer doesn't clear the emotions, I use a tool called "Releasing Attachment." This tool is typically used for clearing heartache or grief when someone has let you down. It also works great for releasing old connections. The process is actually a mantra that said repeatedly will release the attachment you have to a person or thing.

## Releasing Attachment:

Say the following (out loud or silently), over and over, until you feel a sense of calm.

*[name of person, thing, situation]*   I FREE YOU

I RELEASE YOU

I FORGIVE YOU

I LOVE YOU

**Note:** You may not be able to say "I love you" in every situation. If you're extremely angry with someone, "I love you" may be something that's just too much for you to say. Give yourself a break and leave it out if you need to. It's more important to release the emotions that are troubling you than to follow the mantra word for word. When and if you can say "I love you," add it back in. The love I'm speaking of here is unconditional love, and by giving it to others you receive it back for yourself.

**Today's Message:** Can you imagine trying to carry around every possession you have ever owned? Would you carry every pair of shoes, every book, and every toy from your childhood? You readily release physical "stuff," and it's now time to release the emotional and energetic connections to people and memories you have outgrown.

*"Getting over a painful experience is much like crossing monkey bars. You have to let go at some point in order to move forward."*

~ author unknown

# Day 19

## *Be Comfortable with* You

Y ou're an amazing person, and it's high time you know this about yourself! You make your own choices, you create your own life, you have your own quirks and personality traits, and it's time to become comfortable with every aspect of this amazing being. How? you might ask.

Allow yourself to be who you are – nothing more and nothing less. Give yourself a day off from judging *you*. Give yourself a day off from resolutions and self-improvement plans. Give yourself permission to be less than perfect.

We are the "perfect paradox." We're all perfect, just as we are, and we're all imperfect. We shine and we dull. We make mistakes and we make corrections. It's all part of the human experience, and no one experiences life as you do. So be comfortable with you – just as you are.

I remember hearing my friend Bijan Anjomi say, "Whatever you resist – persists." I've found this to be true. If there's something about you that you don't like – that you are always complaining about – it will continue to be part of you because of your resistance. When you surrender to what is, the thing you don't like will either continue to be part of you, or it will leave you.

Think about the people you love. Think about your spouse, your children, and your best friends. There are probably aspects of these loved ones that you look past – little faults you wouldn't change because they're part of who they are. Now ask yourself, "Can I love myself as much as, *or more than*, I love these people?"

It's truly time to be comfortable with all of you – the supposed good and supposed bad. In my truth, there's no good or bad; there just is. Embrace every part of who you are. This doesn't mean that some things about you won't change. It doesn't mean that you won't continue to grow and blossom. But it does mean that you love and embrace who you are today, and every day.

**Today's Message:** "As I embrace the completeness of who I am – the wisdom of my mind, the fullness of my body, the absolute chaos of my surroundings, the love and compassion of my heart, and the curiosity of my soul – I find myself sitting and smiling in a vast pool of wonderment. I like me! I really, really, like me!"

*"Life, I fancy, would very often be insupportable, but for the luxury of self-compassion."*

~ George Robert Gissing

# Day 20

## *Give Power to Others (Allow)*

It's my firm belief that at any particular moment everyone is doing the best they can. Often our best doesn't come off looking very good to those around us. Due to whatever emotions we're feeling or struggles we're going through, our best at that moment is not necessarily us at our *all-time* best.

Therefore, I do my best to allow other people to be who they are, and to meet them where they are. It's their choice whether to walk with me, stay where they are, or walk a completely different path. It's not up to me to determine whether or not they're doing what's best for them. Only they can know what's best for them, and only you can know what's best for you.

I can only "fix" me. My acceptance, allowance, and giving of power to others removes my need to fix others. I can guide my children (well, I could if I had children), I can offer assistance to anyone and everyone, I can do my best to be an example, but I cannot do the fixing work for anyone else.

Obviously my profession is to assist people, whether through coaching, mentoring, energy work, workshops, or my writings. The only way to succeed in my profession is to allow people to be themselves and to insist that they take responsibility for their own life experiences. I'm here to assist and to offer whatever guidance I have.

There are times when I'm guided to help a friend through a tough patch. I might help by loaning them money, giving them a place to stay for a while, or offering discounted healing and coaching. I always check with my higher guidance to ensure that I'm not hurting rather than helping. Sometimes the most loving thing you can do is to say no when someone asks for your help. Sometimes they really need to assert their own power, check with their own guidance, and find their own way out of the maze.

It's not easy to say no, but if your guidance says it's the right thing to do – do it. Always follow your guidance and give other people their own power. They might not like you for a while, or they may never speak to you again, but if you keep an eye on their life, they'll most likely come through it and come out better.

There are those we can assist and they'll never hit bottom. And there are those who absolutely must experience what hitting bottom feels like. Neither path is right or wrong. What's important is knowing that each of us holds the power of our own life. Allow others their power. Don't try to mold someone else into whom you think they should be. Allow them to create their own life.

**Today's Message:** It's disrespectful to assume that other people need your help. It's highly respectful – and loving – to assist those who ask and are willing to assert their own power.

*"God provides the wind, but man must raise the sails."*

~St. Augustine

# Day 21

## *Acknowledge Your Role (in Achievements and Misfortunes)*

Whenever I shine, whenever I hit the ball out of the park, I'm happy, thrilled, and honored to accept that I've contributed to the achievement. When I mess up, however, it's not so easy to accept how I contributed to my failure or misstep.

I see this in children and adults. It seems to be a natural tendency to accept and revel in our accomplishments, but find someone or something else to blame for our failures. Though we have a hand in all of it, we're not 100 percent responsible for any of it. Many of our achievements involve contributions from others – people who led the way and cleared the path. Most of our achievements required a measure of personal focus, determination, and effort, but occasionally our success appears to come from pure, blind luck. The same is true of our failures. No one wins alone and no one fails alone. We all have something to do with whatever is happening in our lives.

I remember driving to work one morning and coming to a traffic light that was about to change to red. I could have sped up just a bit and gone through the intersection, but I stopped just as the light turned red. My car came to a full stop, people started crossing the street, and bam! – a truck ran into the back of my car. The truck was travelling at about thirty miles per hour when it hit me. This all happened within a few seconds, and if I hadn't stopped, the truck would have run the red light. If I had sped up through the yellow light, I would not have been involved in an accident.

Perhaps my misfortune saved a pedestrian from coming to harm, perhaps not. However, my decision to stop, when I could have made it through the intersection before the light turned red, contributed to my car being smashed and my spending several weeks going to a chiropractor.

It's easy to blame it all on the driver of the truck. After all, she didn't even notice the light was red and, yes, she received the legal blame. Yet it adds to our awareness when we notice how we've contributed to a "bad" experience. The awareness allows us to ask, "What could I have done differently? How might I have seen this coming?" This awareness does not excuse the actions of a lawbreaker, but it might assist us with avoiding contact with lawbreakers in the future.

It's never easy to admit to ourselves that we made a choice that did not serve us. I'm not suggesting that we beat ourselves up or that we find fault with ourselves. I'm suggesting that when we're deeply honest with ourselves, we notice that perhaps we did contribute something to a bad situation, and we have the opportunity to not only forgive everyone involved in the situation (including ourselves), but to learn from the experience and adjust how we move forward in life.

I'm now more aware of who's driving behind me and how they're driving. When the light turns yellow, I stop if no one is behind me. I stop if the driver behind me seems to be paying attention. However, if the driver behind me is rushing and not paying attention, and if I can do so safely, I rush through the yellow light. That long-ago accident has made me more conscious of my driving.

**Today's Message:** Give yourself a big pat on the back for your wins, and use your losses to further your awareness. Awareness is always a good thing, even when it doesn't feel so good at the time.

*"A man sooner or later discovers that he is the master-gardener of his soul, the director of his life."*

~James Allen

# Day 22

## *Release Your Guilt*

Today we cover another tricky topic. If I've done something wrong and hurt someone, shouldn't I feel guilty about it? If I don't feel remorse for injuring someone, that would make me a sociopath, wouldn't it? After all, the inability to feel remorse or guilt is one of the characteristics of a sociopath. Don't worry – I'm not asking you to become an unfeeling monster. So what do I mean when I suggest that you release your guilt?

Obviously, if you never felt remorse or guilt, you would have nothing to release. Whenever I have a misstep that causes any sort of harm to another person, of course I feel remorse. Naturally, I examine my actions and motivations to understand why and how this occurred and what I might do differently to prevent a future occurrence. We all make mistakes, and feeling guilty triggers some self-examination and, most often, a positive change in behavior.

I'm not suggesting that you should not feel guilt and remorse. But once guilt is felt, is it a worthwhile emotion to hang on to? If appropriate, it's worthwhile to apologize and perhaps do something to make amends. Once you've examined your actions, motivations, and words, and you've learned your lesson, is there any value in continuing to feel guilty? I honestly don't see any value in holding on to these emotions, and that's why I recommend that you forgive yourself fully, releasing the guilt. I recommend re-reading Lesson #4 and using the Forgiveness Process.

Perhaps you feel guilty about working too much or not spending time with your family and friends. Your guilt might be trying to just get your attention. Look at what is creating the guilty feelings and deal with the situation. In other words, when I suggest you release your guilt, I'm suggesting you take appropriate actions, let it go, and move on with your life. Continuing to feel guilty when there's no way to appease the guilt, or when everything that can be done has been done, weighs you down. Holding on to guilt is not healthy for your mind, spirit, or body.

Now that we've covered releasing guilt when remorse is an appropriate response, let's talk about releasing the need to feel guilty for no appropriate reason. Guilt is the emotional response we feel when we've done something we perceive as bad. As we've already talked about, guilt can be a trigger to examine our behavior. It can also be a trigger to examine our *beliefs*.

Last year I received an email from someone from my past. I don't have a current relationship with this person, but he apparently needed to unload some anger and I was the "lucky" recipient. My initial desire was to write back and defend myself, but I chose to delete the email and let it go. The funny thing is, I felt guilty for not responding. I had taken on a *belief* that not acknowledging his feelings is rude. Yet my guidance was very clear that to respond would only agitate him. The most loving thing I could do was allow him to continue to think that I'm a terrible person, and release my need for his approval and my guilt for not responding.

**Today's Message:** As I said at the beginning, today's topic is a tricky one. But holding on to guilt, shame, and remorse can have terrible consequences for your health and happiness. One of the biggest gifts you can give yourself and those you love is the release of guilt. Feel it. Deal with the situation. Then let it go and move on.

*"If all the world hated you and believed you wicked, while your own conscience approved of you and absolved you from guilt, you would not be without friends."*
~ Charlotte Bronte

# Day 23
## *Embrace What* Is

I can often *accept* what is. I can *allow* people to be who they are. I can *acknowledge* that everyone and everything is in divine order. But to actually *embrace* whatever is showing up in front of me? Hmmm, I need to think about that one.

It's easy to embrace what I see as the good things – the fun stuff. But to embrace heartbreak, physical pain, or the loss of someone or something precious to me? The idea of embracing those things sounds like a difficult assignment.

Most of us have grown up with wonderful teachers who assisted us with embracing the changing seasons, the cycles of nature, and the circle of life and death. As we mourn the loss of summer, we embrace the beauty of fall. As we mourn the death of a loved one, we embrace the new life that's born in another dear one.

Today you're being asked to embrace everything you see for what it is. To gain clarity, I looked up the definition of *embrace*. We tend to use this word in the sense of "to love, to cherish, to take up eagerly." In researching the definition, I found "to take up readily (willingly)." For me, that definition clarifies things.

To take up willingly means to deal with what is, as it is, without resistance. You don't have to like what *is* in order to embrace it. You're not required to pretend that an automobile accident is the most fun way to spend your day. But if you spend your energy bemoaning the auto accident, you'll be too exhausted to effectively deal with the other things you need to deal with.

A high-school friend of mine lived a beautiful example of this recently. She works in the office of a church. There's a school next door, a bus stop outside the office door, and a day-care center in the church. People can easily go in and out of the office, and if she is away from her desk for a few moments, no one would notice someone doing so.

She realized one day that her wallet was missing. She was hoping she had misplaced it, but knew that it might have been stolen. Without resistance, she began checking for activity on her credit cards. Someone had used her Starbucks card, so now she knew that the wallet had been stolen. She filed the police report, contacted the credit agencies, the DMV, her bank, and everyone else that she could think of. She had wonderful conversations with very helpful people. She did all of this in a loving way because that's just the type of woman she is. She didn't yell at God or spend all day crying. She embraced what was and dealt with what had to be dealt with. Having her wallet stolen was simply what showed up for her that day.

Sometimes there's a gift in our misfortune – a lesson to be learned – and sometimes there isn't. But embracing what shows up, dealing with it, and moving on is a tremendous gift to yourself and to everyone around you. Just think of all of the extra energy you'll have if you embrace what is rather than judging it as good or bad, complaining and crying to everyone within earshot about your misfortunes, and so on.

When you *embrace* what is, you have energy left over to imagine new ways of being. You can thrive outside "the system" rather than fighting against it. You can connect to your higher realms and gain guidance and clarity that will assist you and those around you. When you embrace what is – lovingly, willingly, or both – you don't get stuck. You move forward in life.

# Putting Down the Paddles

**Today's Message:** It's not important that you like what shows up today, but it is important that you embrace it, whatever it is, as it is. The sooner you deal with the things you don't like, the sooner you get to play with the things you do. Embrace what is, because all of it is part of your life experience. Live it fully!

*"Your work is to discover your world and then with all your heart, give yourself to it."*

~Buddha

# Day 24

## *Ask Yourself, "What Would I Like to Experience Next?"*

O nce I've become comfortable with myself, accepted where I am now, and embraced what is, I like to ask myself, "What would I like to experience next?"

This can sometimes be confused with setting a goal, but there is a subtle difference. A goal creates an expected outcome, whereas "What would I like to experience next?" creates a direction.

I'm not a big fan of goals. There are times when a goal is the perfect thing for me, but in general goals seem too concrete for my liking. They restrict my movement in much the same way as a girdle restricts my tummy. When I set a goal, I create an expectation of attaining that goal. Whenever I've set a goal and really stuck to that vision, I've attained the goal. But I've often found that what I really wanted wasn't what the goal brought me.

When I ask myself, "What would I like to experience next?" I see a general picture of something. Perhaps it's a picture of me sitting in a bookstore or coffee shop signing copies of my book. Perhaps it's a picture of Wolfgang and me enjoying a nice vacation. Whatever the picture is, if I like it, I say to the universe, "Looks good. Let it happen." Then I go on with whatever I was doing. The book signing and the vacation are not goals, but they sound nice. So I let that, or something better, show up.

# Putting Down the Paddles

When I leave it up to the universe to provide me with the experience I've envisioned, I know that something wonderful is coming my way. If I need to take an action or change direction, I receive guidance to that effect. Sometimes the experience I've envisioned never shows up, but going in the direction of that experience has taken me to wonderful places I would never have envisioned.

To better clarify the difference between s*etting a goal* and *choosing a direction*, consider the following: If I lived in St. Louis, and the picture of what I wanted to experience next was the Gulf of Mexico, I could put my boat into the Mississippi River knowing it flows in that direction. Unless something happens along the way to change my journey, I'll end up in the Gulf of Mexico. However, the river's current might wash me ashore along the way and I may see a new picture that calls to me, causing me to shift direction. I have no goal-induced attachment to getting to the Gulf, so changing direction is no big deal. Knowing me, if the Gulf was my *goal*, I would fight to stay in the river rather than allowing my boat to wash ashore.

Goals work great for most people, and I don't want to discourage you from setting goals if they assist you. You may ask yourself what to experience next, and set a goal. That's awesome!

When I complete a big project or arrive at some sort of crossroads, asking myself what I'd like to experience next is a great way to choose a direction. For me, the direction is all I need.

**Today's Message:** What do you want to experience next? Is it an emotion, a feeling, a place, or a person? Give your order to the universe, and then go in the direction of that experience. You may experience what you envision, or you may find yourself guided into an experience you would never have thought of – one you find even more fulfilling.

*"The greatest thing in this world is not so much where we are, but in what direction we are moving."*

~Oliver Wendell Holmes Jr.

# Day 25
## *Identify Doorways*

I've written in a previous lesson about doing something because it "presented," but to be honest, I don't do everything that presents itself. There just aren't enough hours in the day to take advantage of every opportunity that shows up. As I've been writing these lessons, I've had numerous opportunities to attend writing, publishing, and marketing workshops. Some felt appropriate, so I invested time, energy, and money in them. Others covered topics that I was not quite ready for or didn't feel were appropriate to me, so I allowed them to pass.

Every day I hear or read about wonderful ways to make money or grow your business. If I took advantage of all these business opportunities, I'd be so scattered in my thinking and actions that I would never get anything done. The same is true for social and self-improvement opportunities. There are so many opportunities right now! Just browse the Internet for a few minutes and you'll find a plethora of offers that could be a fit for you.

How do you distinguish between doorways and distractions? This is one key area in which the connection with your higher realms really pays off. Your higher levels will assist you in determining what things are doorways for you.

If you've told the universe that you desire a romantic relationship, and the opportunity presents to join a local singles group, that's a doorway. But if you have several singles events to attend at the same time, how do you choose? Do you choose the one that sounds like the most fun? Yeah, I'd probably go with that. What if these events appear to be equal on the fun factor? Is there one event that provides an opportunity to do something that you've always wanted to try, like learning to ski? Try that one. If you're completely unsure, check your guidance.

Sometimes you're guided to walk through a door that your mind thinks is taking you in the wrong direction. If you feel strongly that your guidance is sending you in this direction, then trust your guidance, go through the door, and sooner or later you'll understand why this was the right move for you. If you're unsure, keep asking for guidance until clarity comes to you.

When it comes to identifying doorways, you get better with practice. Don't get too hung up on it, because you can't make a mistake. If you follow a distraction, it's only a temporary detour. Don't worry. Another doorway will open up that will take you down the path toward your heart's desire. If you're very confused, you might consult with an intuitive or do a reading with angel or tarot cards to gain clarity.

**Today's Message:** We live in an abundant universe, filled with more opportunities than we can make use of. There are plenty for all of us to enjoy! As I learn to identify the doorways that are unique to me, my life becomes simpler, easier, and more enjoyable.

*"No pessimist ever discovered the secret of the stars, or sailed to an uncharted land, or opened a new doorway for the human spirit."*

~ Helen Keller

# Day 26
## *Measure Twice, Cut Once*

In carpentry, if the measurement is incorrect, you risk wasting a piece of wood that has been cut too short or at the wrong angle. Sometimes a bad cut can be fixed, but many times it cannot. Even the corrected cuts cause extra work. So the rule of thumb is to measure twice, cut once.

Yesterday I talked about identifying which opportunities are actually doorways for you, and I mentioned that sometimes a door opens that leads to a major life change. What I didn't talk about was how to deal with an emotionally charged doorway.

When considering a change to your life that's driven by emotion, it's especially important to measure twice, cut once. Perhaps you are already contemplating a major life change, or the door that has opened causes you to consider making a major life change. Whether it's moving across the country, leaving a relationship, changing jobs, enrolling in or dropping out of school – all these changes deserve a little extra contemplation.

When presented with a potential for major change, it's imperative that you pull together all your skills to connect with your higher realms and see what clarity they can give you. When presented with a door to a whole new life, check your guidance, sit with what you hear, go on with your day, then circle back around and check your guidance again.

# Putting Down the Paddles

When you feel like you have clarity, consider what your guidance has shared with you and pay attention to how you feel in your gut. If your gut feels peaceful, or even a bit excited, then it agrees with how you've interpreted your guidance. Follow the guidance and enjoy your new life. If your gut is tight and you have a sense of impending doom, then you may have mistaken your mind chatter for guidance. Check again until your guidance and your gut are in agreement.

What if you can't get your guidance and your gut to agree? Here's a tool I've used when my emotions are running high and the mind chatter just won't quiet down. Whenever I feel that I'm unable to connect clearly with my higher guidance, I say something like the following:

"Father, Mother, God, I command the voice of my ego-mind to be silenced while I commune with my higher realms."

I only command the voice to be silenced during conversations with my higher realms. Requiring this part of my mind to sit inactive for more than a few minutes doesn't actually work well for me. So I word my command as either "for the duration of my conversation with my higher realms," or "for five minutes," or "while I commune with my higher realms." Use whatever wording feels right to you.

The first time I tried this, I was amazed! It actually worked. So I tried it again, and again, until I realized that my ego-mind chatter was perfectly happy to take a break whenever I commanded it to do so.

Please note that I don't ask – I command. I'm usually quite stern when voicing this command, and I make sure to say thank you after I've had the successful connection to my guidance.

I don't have to invoke this command very often. It only comes up when my emotions are running high and I keep getting conflicting messages.

The concept of measure twice, cut once is not a way to question my higher guidance. It's a way to confirm that what I'm hearing is truly guidance and not emotion or wishful thinking.

**Today's Message:** When the guidance you seek concerns major life decisions, it's wise to take the extra step of ensuring that you're truly connected to source and hearing clear guidance. You cannot offend God by ensuring that what you're hearing is truly coming from God.

*"Choose always the way that seems the best, however rough it may be. Custom will soon render it easy and agreeable."*

~Pythagoras

# Day 27

## *Remember that You Cannot Make a Mistake*

$\mathbf{A}$re you getting confused yet? First, I tell you to listen to your higher guidance. But, wait! You might want to double-check that what you're hearing is truly guidance! Oh, don't worry about it – you cannot make a mistake! Is your brain shouting to me, "Make up your mind!"? If so, I can't blame you.

Just what do I mean when I say you cannot make a mistake? We are eternal beings who are spending a short time here in these bodies, on this planet. We each have our own unique reason to be here. But regardless of why we're here, we're each on a unique journey with no absolute destination.

Our time here – our journey – is what is of the utmost importance. Given that we have no concrete destination, it doesn't matter if we travel through life along a straight line or if we take a twisty-turny route with bends and circles, ups and downs. If we truly desire to visit the top of the mountain, we'll get there. It's just a matter of whether we take a direct route or a scenic route. Neither choice is right or wrong.

Why should we concern ourselves with any of this stuff if we cannot make a mistake? The best answer I can give you is the answer that I give to myself: You've chosen a journey of increased

The 30 Lessons

awareness, awakening, and connection; you wouldn't have made it to this point in the book if you weren't on this journey with me.

I ask for guidance because it makes my journey easier. Sure, I can get from Pahrump to Las Vegas by driving the dirt and rock paths up and over Mt. Charleston. It isn't wrong to do so, even if my car is likely to get stuck or damaged. But taking the highway *around* Mt. Charleston is an easier and quicker drive. By following guidance, I can move from experience to experience with more grace and ease.

I encourage you to let go of any attachment you might have to a particular outcome. Often we're so focused on finding our pot of gold at the end of the rainbow that we beat ourselves up for taking the scenic route.

***Today's Message:*** You're here to experience life as fully as possible. When you truly understand this, you'll never make another mistake, and forgiveness, releasing judgments, allowing, and all of the other concepts in these lessons will become a natural part of you.

*"Every moment and every event of every man's life on earth plants something in his soul."*

~Thomas Merton

# Day 28

## *Stop Pushing That Rock up a Hill*

Today's lesson is about surrender. It's about surrendering to your passion, your interests, and your guidance. It's about surrendering to the flow of life.

How many times have you worked very hard at something, only to experience the frustration of taking two steps forward and one step back? Perhaps you're struggling to push a rock up a hill when the rock prefers to stay where it is.

Many things in life deserve concentrated effort. I don't think that life is all about sitting on your couch and expecting the world to come to you. How do I tell when an effort is pushing a rock up a hill and when it's inspired and appropriate? When nothing is working, nothing seems to be flowing, and I feel emotionally exhausted with the effort. When it feels like I'm bumping heads with everyone around me and life feels hard, I realize I'm attempting to push that rock up a hill. It's time for me to take a break, take a breath, and ask for divine assistance.

When I started writing today's lesson, it felt like pushing a rock up a hill. It was not until I surrendered, gave up any attachment to the outcome, walked away from my computer for a while, and then asked for guidance and help that the words began to flow.

If it feels like you're struggling with life, ask yourself a few questions: Are you following your own path, or the path that you believe you're supposed to follow? Are you on the path of *purpose* or the path of *meeting expectations*? Perhaps it's time to surrender to the flow of life.

Suppose you hate your job, or your marriage isn't going well. Am I suggesting that you quit your job or divorce your spouse? *No!* I'm suggesting that you can have a better experience in your job, your marriage, and the other aspects of your life when you surrender to your higher guidance. The guidance may show you a doorway that takes you away from your current job, relationship, house, etc., but rarely does it do so in a drastic way. Surrender to your guidance, not your ego.

When we're pushing a rock up a hill, we have an attachment to the idea that this particular rock must be at the top of this particular hill. We're becoming attached to an outcome and working feverishly toward that outcome. When we stop pushing and take a moment to seek guidance and clarity, we may find an easier way to accomplish what we desire. We may find that the rock we want is already at the top of the hill, but we never bothered to look. Sometimes we realize that we're attempting to push someone else's rock. When that's the case, not only is it time to stop pushing, but it's time to step away altogether. Allow that person to deal with their life in their own way, offering assistance but certainly not doing the pushing for them.

Whenever you feel like you're pushing to make something happen, take a moment to cease your efforts and consider what you really want. What's at the core of your desire? Perhaps there's an easier way for you to achieve your desire. Surrender is the key.

When I surrender to the flow – to my guidance – I get a message about what comes next and I go with it. Sometimes I have to take my boat out of the water and carry it over some rocks and hills to get back to a navigable part of the river. Other times I ride the rapids. Still other times I float smoothly and easily down the river toward whatever life has in store for me next.

# Putting Down the Paddles

**Today's Message:** Whenever it feels like you're pushing, fighting, and clawing your way through the muck and mire – stop. Stop pushing, take a break, and ask for guidance. Ask for help, and help will arrive.

*"The greatness of a man's power is the measure of his surrender."*
~ William Booth

# Day 29
## *Listen*

There are religious orders in which the members devote themselves to silence. They go about their days and nights without speaking a word. My guidance told me that all the knowledge of the universe is contained in a single moment's silence. All that's required for us to gain this knowledge is to listen.

Listening requires a bit of silence and a focus on what's being shared with you. Not speaking is not the same as listening. If you're not speaking, but your mind is full of the words you're planning to speak next, then you're not listening. Listening is a skill that's easy for some, but terribly difficult for others. The first step is the ability to be silent in your mind as well as in your speech.

That sounds so easy, but it's more difficult than it seems on the surface. Have you ever taken a yoga or meditation class and been told to "quiet your mind"? Have you been able to do that? I'm fine for a short time, but before long the mind chatter seems to pop in. I do much better when I'm listening to someone speak because I have their words to concentrate on.

To live in the flow does not require a devotion to silence, but it does require enough silence to allow guidance and wisdom the opportunity to make themselves heard.

How many times have you been speaking with a friend about some problem you have, asked for help, and just kept talking? Your friend might have had some good advice for you, or at least a question that might steer you toward a solution, but you didn't give them an opportunity to assist. You'll never hear a solution if your friend can't get a word in edgewise, as my mother likes to say.

The same is true with your higher levels. If you rage at God about your problems but don't take a moment to listen, you'll never hear the guidance that could move you through those problems into a better life.

Practice listening. Begin by listening to the people who are attempting to connect with you. Then move on to listening to everything around you. Then, most important, practice listening to your higher levels – especially when you've asked for clarity and assistance.

**Today's Message:** All the wisdom and knowledge of the universe is contained in a moment's silence. Practice your listening skills and you'll gain access to the best research library in the universe.

*A wise old owl lived in an oak*
*The more he saw the less he spoke*
*The less he spoke the more he heard*
*Why can't we all be like that wise old bird?*
~ nursery rhyme, author unknown

# Day 30
## *Life Is Good*

L ife is good – because I say so.

Taking things a step further, when I step outside the duality of good versus bad, life just *is*. When I watch the events of my life playing out, as a neutral observer, I sometimes laugh at my perceived misfortunes, and always celebrate every part of this life experience. When I can put aside my personal agenda and allow myself to go with the flow of life, my life falls into alignment with the wisdom of my higher levels.

Here's an example of this alignment: About two years ago, Wolfgang was approached by a friend who offered to sell him a "park model" mobile home (looks like a baby mobile home, licensed as a travel trailer). There had been a fire in the home, and it needed extensive repairs. Therefore, the price was very low. Wolfgang saw the potential in the home and bought it. He did some initial cleaning, taking out the carpet and damaged drywall, but never quite got going on the project.

The home sat in the back of our property for two years until "the flow" brought us Fred. Fred is retired and is a master at repairing and rebuilding homes. He doesn't like to sit around, and the mobile-home project interested him. Wolfgang and Fred are now rebuilding this little house. They've repaired the roof, rebuilt two exterior walls, and fixed several windows and two doors. The wiring is fixed and the drywall is up. The cleaning, painting, and

# Putting Down the Paddles

carpeting are next. Wolfgang could have pushed himself and worked for the past two years on this house, but waiting for the right time has made the job easier and more fun.

When I'm in the flow of life, things take care of themselves. For any project or problem, inspiration and help arrive, resources become available, and everything shows up at the right time. It's only my judgment that creates any problems.

Yes, there are days when that judgment runs wild! There are days when I see problems and misfortunes all around me. There are days when nothing seems to be working, my body is sick, and my emotions are running out of control. Is life good on those days? Absolutely, yes!

Today's Message: There's no viable alternative to life, so you might as well enjoy your time here. Don't see death as an alternative to life, but rather as the next grand adventure. You can observe life from a positive, negative, or neutral position. Regardless of your position, life is good!

*"Life is really simple, but we insist on making it complicated."*

~ Confucius

# WRAP-UP

I hope you've enjoyed this 30-day journey. I'll be the first to say that living in the flow is not always easy, and can often be very uncomfortable. Striving to achieve goals and competing to win are just two programs that are deeply ingrained in the consciousness of most westerners. Having the courage to take a long look at your beliefs and behaviors is to be commended. Congratulations on taking this step toward living your life in alignment with the divine flow of the universe!

Don't stop here. Live these lessons for another 30 days and you will discover deeper meaning and a bit more connection to the flow. Live these lessons for as many 30-day increments as you desire, knowing that each month will bring you more awareness, clarity, and ease.

For readers of this book, I offer a *free* download of *Woo-Woo Wisdom: Inspirational Stories to Transform Your Life*. This PDF-format book contains some of my favorite "Weekly Wisdom" articles paired with favorite photos. Follow this URL to get your download now: www.PuttingDownThePaddles.com/readersonly.html.

Also, as a gift to my readers, I've attached an appendix with my previously published *Tools for Living in the Flow*. You'll recognize some of these tools from their associated daily lesson, while others will be new to you.

As I mentioned in the beginning of this book, I've created a website page where readers can post their thoughts, ask questions, and read through the Frequently Asked Questions (FAQ). I'll update the FAQ periodically based on your questions and feedback. This will give you a place to take your experience "beyond the book." You can find this page by going to www.PuttingDownThePaddles. com/faq.html.

If this is the end of our journey together, I wish you much happiness and success on your path. If you choose to travel with me a while longer, I look forward to connecting with you as a coaching client, at a workshop, or at a book-signing event.

Sending you much love and light,


Susan M. Wright
www.beacon-of-life.com
www.puttingdownthepaddles.com

# APPENDIX

## *Tools for Living in the Flow*

**(Originally published as a stand-alone booklet, copyright 2011.)**

Putting Down the Paddles

## THE BLISS BUBBLE

### What is a Bliss Bubble?:

When I think of the Bliss Bubble, I envision a scene from Star Trek. The captain is on the bridge and an enemy is on his screen. The captain gives the command "Shields up!" and the entire ship is protected by an invisible force field. Missiles shot at the ship cannot penetrate this invisible shield, though productive communications can.

The Bliss Bubble is a form of personal shield – an energetic field surrounding my body that allows only love and light to penetrate it. Only love and light can come into the bubble, and only love and light can go out.

### When to Use the Bubble:

Anytime you're going into a situation in which you might feel attacked, judged, or vulnerable is a good time to use the Bliss Bubble. It's great for situations requiring negotiation skills, because it helps you to stay in peace and keep your cool. For many people, it's also a wonderful tool to use at family functions and professional meetings. Anytime you find yourself desiring a bit of divine protection, just invoke the Bliss Bubble and watch the energies shift.

### Benefits of this Tool:

Using this tool in my life, I notice that hurtful comments or cheap shots lose their bite. Sometimes I don't even hear the comment! My friends will say something to me afterwards about whatever was said, and I honestly hadn't heard it. I've also found that when less-than-kind words (or "ego-comments," as I like to call them) come out of my mouth, other people don't seem to hear them. When I realize that my comments went unnoticed, I silently say, "Thank you for the Bliss Bubble." I bless the conversation and move on in love and light.

I love the Bliss Bubble because it benefits everyone, not just me. By invoking the Bliss Bubble, I set a clear intention to move forward in love; I'm ready to see and hear love, and to speak and act in love.

### Invoking the Bliss Bubble:

Envision a shield around your body, like an invisible bubble with you at its center. Command that only love and light can move through this shield. Only love and light can come in, and only love and light can go out.

### For example:

*"Father, Mother, God, I command that only love and light can come in through this shield, and that I emanate only love and light to everyone and everything around me. Thank you, God. It is done."*

Now, go forward in perfect peace!

## Food Blessing

Young children often bless their food by saying whatever comes into their heads at that moment. This has been such a heart-warming experience for me that I have adopted their style.

When I sit down to a meal, I bless all the animals, plants, and people who have contributed to my meal, while also sending love to mother earth. When I experience discomfort in my body, I ask the food to heal these pains and aches.

I woke up one morning with a headache, and instead of taking an aspirin, I blessed my breakfast and asked it to heal the headache. By the time I finished eating, the headache was gone.

Some people are very concerned about chemicals and contaminates in their food. If this is a concern for you, you can also command that your body take what it requires from your food and allow the rest to pass through, causing no harm to you or your body.

You can hold your hands over your plate when blessing your food as a visual signal to your brain; you can say your blessing out load or you can say your blessing silently.

### An Example:

*Father, Mother, God, Bless this meal, and all of the people, plants, and animals that have contributed to it. Thank you for bringing this divine sustenance to me, and may this sustenance bring healing and health to my body, and may my body easily pass through all that it does not need or desire for highest health and well-being.*

## ALLOWING

I allow everybody in my life to do whatever they want to do, and I reserve the right for me to do whatever I want to do, when and with whom I want to do it. This includes allowing my current boyfriend to do what he wants, when and with whom he wants.

Obviously, this one can be tricky. On the surface it sounds like I'm taking a position that allows others to walk all over me. But that's not what I'm saying.

*Allowing* gives everyone the choice to live as they wish. If someone chooses to dishonor you, it is your choice to accept the mistreatment or to walk away from it.

It's one thing to say, "I will not allow you to do this." It's quite another to say, "If you choose to do this, I will choose to be somewhere other than where you are." The first statement is an attempt to control the person. The second statement makes it clear that you are setting a personal boundary. Setting and maintaining your boundaries is a very healthy thing to do. Attempting to control another person is not only very difficult, but can lead to disappointment, anger, resentment, and other unhealthy emotions.

Allowing does not cancel out the laws of cause and effect, nor does it exempt parents or guardians from the job of guiding and raising their children.

*Always* follow your heart, your gut, and your higher guidance when deciding how best to *allow*.

## The Best Day of My Life

Often when I'm asked, "How are you today?" my response is, "Today is the best day of my life!"

Many people look at me funny when I make this statement, but here's my reasoning: Yesterday is gone, tomorrow is not yet here, so today is the only day I really have.

On top of that, the present moment is the only time that's truly real to me. Today is my day for me – my choice for me – no matter what goes on in the world. I can always find plenty of reasons why today is the best day of my life.

One benefit of living this way is that it helps me live life in the present moment.

So how is my life now? ...The Best!

## My Life Is in the Flow

Watching a mountain stream, I noticed that water is always flowing from a higher elevation to a lower level. Water flows easily; it doesn't fight the flow. Water doesn't complain about the unfairness of the boulder in its path; it flows around the boulder.

This is how, to the best of my ability, I live my life. I go with the flow of what presents itself, what shows up. If there's something I desire to have in my life, I ask my higher self, God, and the universe to provide me with what I want – and then I go on about my life. I don't focus on the desire. I deal with whatever shows up. If what I desire shows up, I thank God. If not, it's not a big deal – especially when I consider all the bounty in my life. Often what does appear in my life is so much more joyful than what I had desired that I find it easy to see and respect the wisdom of my higher levels.

My relationship with Wolfgang "showed up." I had desired a relationship, and had been putting a lot of focus on that. When I gave up and put my focus on what was already in my life, suddenly Wolfgang showed up, and I could not have asked for a more compatible partner. Thank you, God.

The same is true for my business, my health, and every other aspect of my life. Opportunities present themselves to me and I go with those that feel appropriate. I no longer analyze and evaluate every detail of every situation. I get a sense of what is right for me and I go with that.

Life gets better every day, and I really enjoy looking downstream and around the next bend to see what's going to happen next. I've tried paddling upstream, fighting the current and pushing to make things happen. I much prefer dealing with what shows up right in front of me and then moving on. I'm enjoying the flow of life!

## THE TO-DO LIST (WITH A TWIST)

### What It Is:

As I set up my day, I often write out a to-do list of all the things I want to accomplish that day. I find that my head feels clear and open for guidance once the list is done. As more items present, I add them to the list. As items are completed, I check them off. This allows my mind to stay clear all day.

Recently I started a second to-do list. It lists all the things that I'm allowing Spirit, God, and my higher self to handle. I only take an action on these when I feel inspired to do so.

For example, my daily to-do list might include:

☐ Post office

☐ Bank

☐ Groceries

☐ Gas station

# Putting Down the Paddles

While my higher self to-do list might show:

- ❏ Abundant money flow

- ❏ Optimal health

- ❏ Loving, effortless relationships

- ❏ Writing my book

- ❏ Finding the best builder for my new house

When I use this tool, my mind only needs to decide on the proper list for each task. At any given moment a task may present itself to me, and I simply add it to one of these to-do lists. This allows me to always be clear and open for divine guidance.

Life is good.

Life is easy.

Life is fun.

When my mind brings up an issue from the "higher self" list and wants to worry about it, I gently remind my mind that the issue is on the list and it will be taken care of. I remind myself of examples from the past when my higher self took excellent care of an issue, and this tends to quiet my mind.

## THE FORGIVENESS PROCESS

### What It Is:

I believe that everyone and everything is perfect. I know that whatever comes into my life is there for a reason. Ultimately, I know that there's nothing to forgive – and yet I make good use of the Forgiveness Process. The Forgiveness Process is a way to invoke universal forgiveness and divine grace. I've seen severe situations shift and heal completely simply by using this process.

### When to Use It:

The perfect time for the Forgiveness Process is when you feel that someone has done something to you.

### A Couple of Mild Examples *(severe situations would take pages to share):*

A new acquaintance invited me to a pot-luck get together. When I arrived, I felt very uncomfortable. Everyone there was much younger than me and dressed very differently from me, and I found myself creating judgments about them. As I poured myself a diet soda, I silently did the Forgiveness Process for everyone there. When I turned back to the party, I found myself engaging in a wonderful conversation with one of the women whom I had judged. We had much in common, and I could now see everyone there in a loving way.

While wrapping up a three-day training event, a woman made a comment to me that was quite hurtful. The funny thing was, she thought she was complimenting me. As soon as I had a moment, I excused myself from the room and found a quiet spot to do the Forgiveness Process. Afterward, I was able to give this woman a truly warm hug goodbye. I no longer felt pain from her comment, and was able to acknowledge her contribution to the weekend.

This process works miracles for family gatherings and is a perfect relationship tool!

# Putting Down the Paddles

I believe it works because it shifts my energy toward others and helps me remain calm and peaceful. It clears feelings of resentment, anger, jealousy, or victimhood.

**The Process** *(can be used with individuals or groups of any size):*

Say the following (out loud or silently):

> Father, Mother, God,
> I forgive _____ for everything they have ever done
> For everything they are doing now
> And for everything they will ever do.
> AND
> I *(ask or command)* _____ to forgive me
> For everything that I have ever done
> For everything that I am doing now
> And for everything that I will ever do.
> Thank you, God.
> It is done.

In this process, I like to use "command" in the second part, but some people are not comfortable with such strong wording. "Ask" works just as well, since what you're doing is shifting *your* energy.

## RELEASING ATTACHMENT

This process came to me when I was counseling a close friend. She was dealing with a very uncomfortable situation. Each time she saw a particular person, she felt anger, resentment, sadness, grieving, and other damaging emotions well up inside of her. The emotions were making her physically ill. I comforted her as best I could and suggested a mantra. It was one of those moments when I heard words coming from my mouth and thought, "Wow, this sounds profound. I wonder where this came from?" Clearly this was not my rational mind speaking. This was information coming directly through me from higher powers. The funny thing is, after our conversation I completely forgot what I had suggested to her.

A couple of months later I was speaking with my friend and she told me, "That thing you told me to do worked wonders! I've been using it every time those emotions come up, and now there's hardly any emotion at all. I've really let that person go and I feel much better!"

For the life of me, I could not remember what I had told her, so I asked her. This time, I wrote it down so I could share it with others.

What I have found by using this process myself and by receiving feedback from others is that it has a wide range of uses. The more something is bugging you, the more you say the mantra. Anytime I feel myself attached to someone or something, I use this mantra. I'm amazed at the results! The knot in my stomach disappears and I return to peace and calm.

Attachment is a funny thing. As long as everything is moving along smoothly and the other person / thing / situation is filling whatever gap you want them to fill – all is well. The trouble arises when the inevitable happens – that gap is no longer filled. You feel abandoned. The attachment has prevented you from becoming a whole person. When you are whole and complete, as yourself, then you have no need for something or someone to fulfill you; you free yourself to fully enjoy your relationships, your possessions, and your life situations without depending upon any of these to complete you.

# Putting Down the Paddles

**What It Is:**

This process is actually a mantra that, when said repeatedly, will release the attachment that you have to a person or thing.

Releasing attachment does *not* mean that this person or thing is no longer in your life. What it means is that you no longer feel dependent upon this person or thing for your happiness, health, or well-being.

**When to Use It:**

- When someone has broken your heart or let you down.
- When you find yourself saying, "I don't know what I would do without X."
- When you find yourself being overly protective of a possession, such as your car.
- When the sight of someone, or even the mention of their name, causes you emotional pain.
- When you worry about losing something.

**The Process:**

Say the following (out loud or silently), over and over, until you feel a sense of calm:

[*name of person, thing, situation*]  I FREE YOU

I RELEASE YOU

I FORGIVE YOU

I LOVE YOU

**Note:** You may not be able to say "I love you" in every situation. If you're extremely angry with someone, "I love you" may be too much for you to say. Give yourself a break and leave it out if you have to. It's more important that you release the emotions that are troubling you than to follow the mantra word for word. When, and if, you can say "I love you," add it back in. The love I'm speaking of here is unconditional love, and by giving it to others you receive it back for yourself.

## DISCONNECTING

*What It Is:*

Disconnecting is a way to bring yourself out of the past, out of the future, and back to who and what is with you in this present moment.

*When to Use It:*

As I go through my day, speaking with many people about many different things, I sometimes find that people or events continue to pop up in my mind. Similar to the pop-ups on a computer screen, these thought pop-ups can be very distracting. I like to be in the here-and-now, and a constant stream of pop-ups prevents that.

Anytime you find yourself lost in thoughts about people who are not currently with you or events that are not currently happening, you can disconnect.

*The Process:*

I use the following prayer as a way to disconnect:

Archangel Michael,
Bathe me in the blue light protection of God
And with your blazing sword cut all of my connections
To everyone and everything.
Burn root, branch, and seed of every negative connection I have
And leave everyone and everything blessed.
Thank you, Michael.
It is done.

Putting Down the Paddles

## THE CLEARING PROCESS

### What It Is:

This is a process you can use to clear and release emotions, beliefs, and other energies that are no longer serving you. This process clears and releases these energies from your body, your etheric bodies (also referred to as your energetic bodies, or aura), your DNA, and all dimensions where your spirit may be currently residing.

### When to Use It:

Whenever you notice that you have a belief, fear, or judgment that's no longer serving you, or when someone or something upsets or irritates you, you have a choice. Your first choice is to keep this belief, experience being upset and irritated, and enjoy it fully. Or you can use this opportunity to release these beliefs, emotions, or any other negative energy that's presenting to you in that moment. Of course, it's also possible to do both. Often after fully experiencing the emotion, you decide you don't want to experience it again. In that case, you can use the clearing process after the emotions have subsided.

When I'm very emotional and not able to focus fully on the clearing for myself, I ask a friend to do this process with me. The emotional support of a friend assisting me with the clearing makes it much easier to fully release the emotions.

### The Process:

Give yourself a quiet moment. Sit or lie quietly, close your eyes, and relax. Say (aloud or in your mind):

Father, Mother, God,
Creator of all that is,
I command a healing for myself.
I command to pull and release all the emotions, beliefs, and energies that are presenting regarding _____. I command

to pull and release these from all my bodies (mental, emotional, physical, and etheric) and from all my dimensions, resolving them in my past and clearing them from all my futures. I command to pull and release all roots and anchors that may be holding these energies within me, and to clear these energies from my DNA.

Thank you, God.

It is done.

Now pay attention to what's happening inside your body. You may feel energy moving, and you may feel a need to cough or breathe deeply. Your body may feel a need to shake or rock. Just allow whatever happens. It's a sign that the energies are moving and releasing from your being.

Periodically ask, "Is this process complete?" Listen to your inner voice and you'll hear either a yes or a no. It's preferable to wait until you hear yes to go about your day. However, there may be instances when the clearing takes hours or even days. If you need to go on about your day, simply command that the clearing continue until it's complete (similar to a computer program running in the background). I visualize an "Auto Clear" button and turn it on so that I can go on with my day.

## TOOLS WRAP-UP

There you have it – a small collection of tools that just might make a very big difference in how you enjoy your life. These tools have had a very positive impact on my life and the lives of my clients and friends.

I was once asked if using these tools means that I'm always happy, healthy, and in peace. The short answer would be no. There are still things in my life that cause me emotional distress. However, these tools help me find my way out of the distress and back to a place of peace.

There's nothing wrong with drama, anger, or upset. They're simply emotional states that humans experience, like happiness, joy, and peace. And yet it's our choice to remain in those emotional states or to move through them. I like being happy, so I usually choose to move through unhappiness as gracefully as I possibly can.

As I mentioned in the wrap-up to the lessons, I've created a page on my website where readers can post their thoughts, ask questions, and read through the Frequently Asked Questions (FAQ). I'll update the FAQ periodically based on your questions and feedback. This will give you a place to take your experience "beyond the book." You can find that group by going to www.PuttingDownThePaddles.com/faq.html.

Enjoy your 30-day journey as often as you like, and experience the freedom of putting down your paddles and letting the river take you where it may.

Sending you much love and light,

*Susan M. Wright*
www.beacon-of-life.com
www.puttingdownthepaddles.com

# ACKNOWLEDGMENTS

Thank you to those who helped me create this beautiful life in the flow.

Thank you, Wolfgang, for allowing me to be whoever I need to be at any given time. Thanks for your patience and support through this book-writing process, and always.

Many thanks to my parents, who encouraged me to learn, challenge, and always follow my heart. Dad, I miss you. Mom, I love you.

Thank you to my supportive and helpful "unpaid book squad," Michael, Sue A., Sue C., Amy, Peggy, Stephanie, Karen, Joe, Melinda, and Mary Kay. Your questions, comments, and suggestions were a great help – and your love and support were, and are, invaluable.

To my family, friends, teachers, healers, clients, students, fellow coaches, fellow healers, and fellow writers, you have each inspired me in ways that are too numerous to list here. For all you have given me, I give you my deep appreciation.

## ABOUT THE AUTHOR

Susan M. Wright is the owner and founder of Beacon Of Life®, a life coaching company dedicated to "Lighting the Way to Your Life in the Flow." Susan began her coaching career after taking early retirement from her corporate career. She is a life coach, author, ordained metaphysician with Lightworker.com, and energy healer. After ten years of working with clients and continuing to study, grow, and evolve, Susan wrote this book as a way to share these lessons with a wider audience.

If you have any questions about what you have read or about Susan's services, you can contact her at susan@beacon-of-life.com, or peruse her website: www.beacon-of-life.com.

### ADDITIONAL SERVICES FROM SUSAN M. WRIGHT AND BEACON OF LIFE®

#### "Weekly Wisdom"

"Weekly Wisdom" is a *free* weekly e-newsletter, delivered directly to your email inbox each Sunday morning. Each weekly article shares life experiences and ideas to assist you in seeing life from a different perspective. Sign up for "Weekly Wisdom" at: www.beacon-of-life.com.

#### Infusion of Love®

*A Transformational Experience*

Infusion of Love® is a one-on-one session, either in person or over the phone, that creates a space for love from your higher realms to transform your life. In other words, an energy healing service to assist quantum transformation, eliminate stress, and assist you with living life more fully.

## Life and Relationship Coaching

Just as a sports coach assists the athlete with playing their best game, a life coach assists their clients with playing their best "game of life." Working one-on-one, or in a group coaching situation, Susan assists her clients with embracing their talents and learning to live in their own unique flow of life, all while creating and maintaining high-quality personal and professional relationships.

## Digital Coaching

Digital Coaching is perfect for the client who has a simple question and is most comfortable with email. Clients email their question or concern, and Susan responds by email (typically within one business day). This is the perfect low-cost service for anyone wanting a new perspective on a particular situation. Digital Coaching is not meant to replace traditional coaching.

To sign up for "Weekly Wisdom," and to get more information on the services provided by Beacon Of Life®, visit Susan's website at: www.beacon-of-life.com.